CHAPTER 1
Tools

Tools help you to mold and shape your fabric into finished pieces. Like a sculptor with clay, you too must encourage the fabric to take a shape other than its own, transforming it from a formless state into a recognizable creation. Every cut, every mark that you make brings you one step closer to the realization of your creative vision.

Cutting Tools

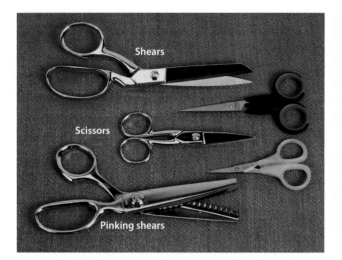

Shears

Scissors

Pinking shears

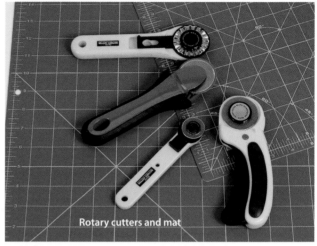

Rotary cutters and mat

Shears

Ideal for cutting out fabric, shears have blades longer than 6" and two different-sized handle bows or loops (a smaller opening for the thumb; a larger opening for two or more fingers). Some shears have bent handles that keep the fabric flat when you're cutting, making it easy to cut straight, accurate lines. Buy the best quality shears you can afford. Take good care of them and they'll last for a lifetime of good sewing.

Pinking Shears and Scallop Shears

Use pinking and scallop shears primarily for creating decorative finishes on no-fray fabrics such as oilcloth and synthetic suede. Pinking shears cut a zigzag edge. Scallop shears cut a rounded, scalloped edge.

Scissors

Scissors have blades less than 6" long and identical handle bows for the finger and thumb. Used mainly for clipping threads and trimming seams, they're also great for crafts.

Motivating Memo Caring for cutting tools
properly is important to make them last longer and
work better. Here are some guidelines:
- **If the blades become dull, have them sharpened.**
- **Don't drop scissors, shears, or rotary cutters. This could**
  damage the blades or make it difficult to cut accurate, crisp
  lines on the fabric.
- **To keep the blades sharp longer, use your shears, scissors,**
  and rotary cutters only for sewing.

Rotary Cutter and Cutting Mat

A rotary cutter, originally designed for quilt making, looks and works like a pizza cutter. The round razor-like blade at the end of the handle is retractable when not in use and is replaceable. Remember to cover or retract the blade when not in use to avoid injury.

Rotary cutters are available in many sizes. Use the larger size for cutting straight edges or heavier fabric. Save the smaller cutters for cutting out pattern pieces on light- to mid-weight fabrics – they provide greater maneuverability around curved areas than larger ones.

You must use a cutting mat with a rotary cutter. The mat/cutter duo is perfect for accurately cutting several layers of fabric and for protecting your work surface. The gridded ruler on the mat is very helpful. Choose a mat with precise grid markings.

Cutting mats are made of "self-healing" material that is not damaged by the rotary cutter blade.

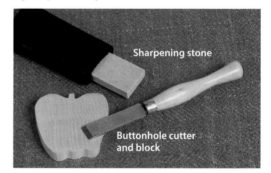

Sharpening stone

Buttonhole cutter and block

Buttonhole Cutter, Block, and Sharpening Stone

Use a buttonhole cutter and block to open stitched buttonholes for a professional look. The cutter has a hardwood handle and a hardened steel blade; the wooden block comes in various shapes.

A sharpening stone is useful for maintaining quality sewing shears and scissors. Use the stone to sharpen the blades periodically to ensure clean-cut edges. Slide the stone upward along the beveled surface of the knife edge blade, working from the tip of the blade to the shank. After honing, wipe the blade clean.

Sew
with
confidence

A beginner's guide to basic sewing

© 2004 Nancy Zieman

Published by

krause publications
An imprint of F+W Publications, Inc.

700 East State Street • Iola, WI 54990-0001
715-445-2214 • 888-457-2873
www.krause.com

Our toll-free number to place an order or obtain
a free catalog is (800) 258-0929.

The following company or product names appear in this book:
Bamboo Pointer and Creaser, Chacopel, Chaco-Liner, EZ Feeder Guide, Ezy-Hem® Gauge by Dritz,
Fasturn®, Fine Fuse®, Fix Velour®, Fray Check™, Fusible Tricot, Iron Quick, Jeans Stitch Thread, Jet-Air
Threading Serger, Lightweight Pellon®, Little Wooden Iron, Omnigrid, Pellon® Bi-Stretch Lite™, Pocket
Curve Template, Sewer's Fix-It Tape, Stacy's®, Shape Flex, Teflon™, ThreadFuse, Triangle Tailor's Chalk,
Velcro®, Whisper Weft™, Wonder-Under™

Library of Congress Catalog Number: 2004093874

ISBN: 0-87349-811-9

Edited by Barbara Case
Designed by Marilyn McGrane
Illustrations by Laure Noe
Photographs by Dale Hall

Printed in the United States of America

Table of Contents

Introduction

Congratulations. You have in your hands the one and only book you will need to lead you to success as a sewer.

Many of you will know me from my television show, "Sewing With Nancy," and from ordering supplies from Nancy's Notions. I began sewing when I was 7 and have that first apron to prove it. Yes, I've advanced to sewing jackets, blazers, appliquéd garments and dozens of more difficult projects. But we all started at the beginning. And that's what this book does.

Inside these pages you will find all the information you need to become a successful sewer. We begin with the selection of tools and fabrics. Then we start sewing. You'll find step-by-step instructions for installing zippers and constructing sleeves. We even show you how to make pillows, curtains and gift bags.

And along the way I'll share some motivating messages and tips of the trade.

So, let's get sewing.

Regards,

Nancy Zieman

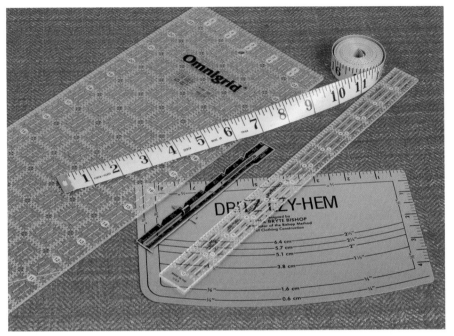

Top to bottom: An Omnigrid ruler, a tape measure, 6" hem gauge, a ruler, and an Ezy-Hem Gauge.

Tape Measure

Use a tape measure when measuring larger items such as the fabric grainline and to determine the pattern size. Choose a 60" long tape made of durable, nonstretching material with metal or plastic tips on the ends to protect them from fraying. Look for a tape measure that has markings on both sides, in both metric and American measurements.

6" Hem Gauge

Useful for smaller measuring jobs, a 6" sewing gauge has a double-pointed slide to guide you in marking hems, pleats, buttons, and buttonhole placements. The sliding pointer makes it easy to get even measurements.

Ruler

A heavyweight, transparent plastic ruler marked with accurate horizontal and vertical lines is a must for ease in measuring when working with a rotary cutter and mat. Gridded rulers are available in a wide variety of sizes. Having measurements marked in both yellow and black is helpful. The dual markings make it easy to measure on both light and dark fabrics.

Ezy-Hem Gauge

Use this lightweight metal gauge to mold straight or curved hems while measuring accurately, in one easy step. The gauge also prevents pressing over the cut edge of the hem, which could leave an imprint on the right side of the fabric.

Marking Tools

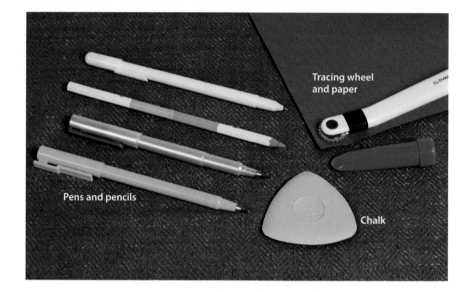

Marking Pens and Pencils

Fabric marking pens are available in air- and water-soluble forms. Air-soluble pens (generally with purple ink) contain disappearing ink that vanishes within 12 to 24 hours. Water-soluble pens (generally with blue ink) contain ink that can be removed with cold water.

Fabric marking pencils have super-thin lead specifically designed for fabric. Since they contain less graphite than standard pencil leads, they resist smearing and washing out. Marks erase with a drop of cold water. Pencils are also available with white lead for marking dark fabrics.

Do not use regular ballpoint pens or regular lead pencils, as their marks are difficult to remove.

Chalk

Chalk comes in several forms and is available in several colors to contrast with every fabric.

- **Chaco-Liner** looks similar to a tube of lipstick. It dispenses in accurate, thin powder lines on any fabric. Chaco-Liners are available in white, pink, yellow, or blue for light and dark fabrics.
- **Triangle Tailor's Chalk** has a chalk base in a firm triangular form. Triangles come in yellow, white, red, and blue, and they never leave a stain.
- **Chacopel Pencils** are tailor's chalk in the form of fine line pencils. Chalk marks brush or wash out easily. These come in white, yellow, and pink/blue. Pencil caps with brushes and a sharpener are also available.

Tracing Wheel and Paper

Tracing wheels may have pointed (serrated), scalloped, or smooth edges. Serrated edges make a dotted line and may leave holes in the pattern. Scalloped edges make a dashed line, which puts more marks on the fabric. Smooth edges make a solid line, which also puts more marks on the fabric. Use special sewing tracing paper in the lightest color that will show on your fabric and try to mark on the wrong side, as the marks may be difficult to remove.

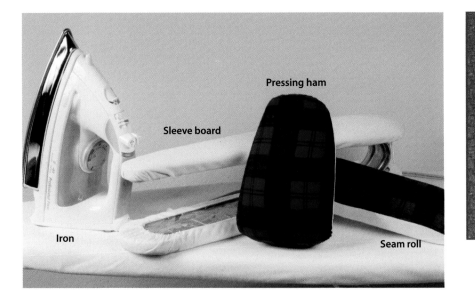

Iron · Sleeve board · Pressing ham · Seam roll

Iron and Ironing Board

You'll use an iron to press every seam you sew. Choose an iron that can be used as either a steam iron or a dry iron. After you finish sewing and pressing, *always* turn off and unplug the iron and empty the water from a steam iron.

Ironing boards come in several sizes. Look for an ironing board that you can adjust up and down for use when standing or sitting, making it more comfortable to iron and press. Attach a bag or basket to hold scraps and trimmed threads.

Sleeve Board

A sleeve board has a free arm for pressing small openings and hard to reach areas such as sleeves and pant legs.

Seam Roll

Use a seam roll to press open seams. The rounded surface of a seam roll prevents the imprint of the seam edges from showing on the right side of the fabric. You can make a seam roll by tightly rolling and taping a magazine and covering it with fabric or a terry towel.

Pressing Ham

A pressing ham has a larger curved surface. Use a ham to press curved areas such as darts or curved seams so they keep their shape.

Press Cloth

A press cloth is a piece of lightweight fabric that you place between the iron and fabric before pressing. It protects the fabric surface from damage and keeps the bottom of the iron clean when fusing.

Iron Cleaner

Use iron cleaner regularly to remove sticky buildup from your iron. Follow the instructions on the product packaging. Regular cleaning will prolong the life of the iron and keep it performing well.

Spray Bottle

This useful notion comes in very handy when pressing. Fill it with water and keep it handy for all pressing jobs. If your iron doesn't produce adequate steam, cover the fabric with a press cloth, mist the press cloth using a spray bottle, and press.

Iron cleaner · Press cloth

Sewing Tools

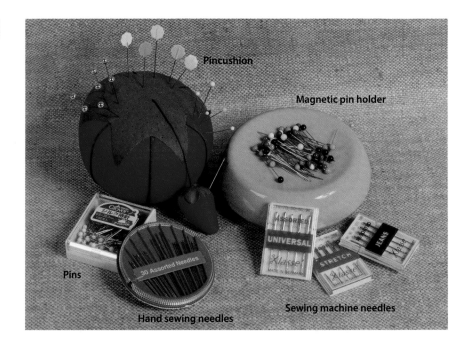

Pincushion

Magnetic pin holder

Pins

Hand sewing needles

Sewing machine needles

Sewing Machine Needles

Sewing machine needles come in a variety of sizes and types. The shape of the point differs from type to type, the shape and size of the eye may change, and the needle thickness varies, too. The larger the size of the needle, the thicker it is. For example, a size 90 needle is heavier than a size 80 needle. Use a size 70 or 80 needle for sewing most cottons and blends.

Choose the size and type of needle appropriate for both the fabric and thread you're using and the type of sewing you plan to do. Do some test stitching on a fabric scrap before stitching on your project. Don't hesitate to change needle size or type if your test stitching shows that the needle in your machine makes holes that are too large or if your machine skips stitches.

You'll use the following types of needles most often.

- **Universal**. The point on a universal needle is a blend of sharp and ballpoint, making it suitable for many types of fabric. Use a size 70 or 80 universal to stitch knit and woven fabrics, as well as most cottons and blends. Use a size 90 or 100 for heavier fabrics such as denim or canvas.
- **Stretch**. The rounded ballpoint tip of a stretch needle gently spreads knit fibers apart rather than piercing them. Use a size 75 to stitch lightweight knits.
- **Denim/sharp**. A denim/sharp is a strong needle with a sharp point that pierces tightly woven fabric. Use it to stitch multiple layers of denim or similar fabrics such as canvas.

Hand Sewing Needles

Hand sewing needles come in several different styles and in sizes 3 to 10. Unlike sewing machine needles, the larger the number of a hand sewing needle, the finer it is. For example, a size 10 hand sewing needle is finer than a size 8 needle. Choose the smallest needle (a higher number) that will go through your fabric without bending or breaking.

- **Sharps**. The most commonly used general-purpose hand sewing needles, sharps have round eyes and sharp points.
- **Ballpoint**. The rounded point of a ballpoint needle pushes between fabric yarns instead of piercing them, making them ideal for sewing knits.
- **Crewel**. The long eye of a crewel needle makes it easier to thread than sharps. Crewel needles also accommodate several strands of floss or thread for decorative handwork.

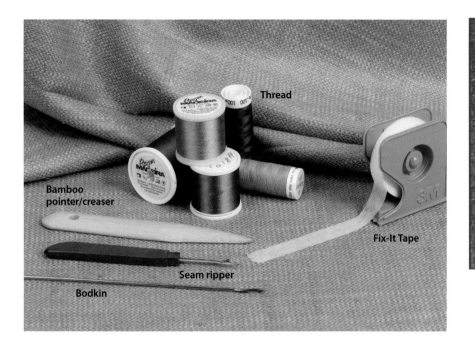

Thread

Bamboo pointer/creaser

Fix-It Tape

Seam ripper

Bodkin

Pins

Necessary for any sewing project, straight pins come in a variety of lengths and diameters. A smaller diameter pin will not leave large holes in your fabric. For basic sewing, use pins with glass or plastic heads. These are gentle on the fingertips and are easy to see and pick up. Glass heads won't melt, but the heat of the iron might melt plastic heads, so be sure to remove them before pressing your project.

Pincushion/Magnetic Pin Holder

The most popular stuffed pincushion is tomato-shaped with a strawberry emery. Pass needles and pins through the emery to sharpen and clean them.

Magnetic pin holders come in a variety of shapes and sizes, including ones you can wear on your wrist while sewing. They are handy for picking up dropped pins and needles.

Seam Ripper

Used for removing stitching mistakes, a seam ripper has a special sharp point that slides under and cuts the thread. Be careful to insert the sharp cutting edge only under the thread used to stitch the seam, *not* under the fabric threads.

Bamboo Pointer and Creaser

Use the pointed end of this tool for turning collars, cuffs, lapels, and appliqués. Use the curved beveled end for temporarily pressing seams open or shaping curved edges (for example, on a round pillow).

Thread

You will most often use basic all-purpose thread made of cotton-covered polyester or 100 percent polyester for machine sewing. Available in a wide variety of colors, this thread works with all types of fabrics for all-purpose sewing.

When choosing thread, take a piece of your fabric to the store. Thread looks slightly darker on the spool than it will when you sew with it. Select a thread color that's slightly darker than the fabric.

There are many threads available for special uses such as embroidery, quilting, topstitching, metallic, invisible, fusible, and many more. Try these threads when you have more experience.

Sewer's Fix-It Tape

This easy to remove tape is an essential and versatile sewing tool. Use it to tape patterns. You can write on it and iron over it, and the pattern remains tissue soft. It also works as a 1/2" stitching guide when inserting zippers, and you can use it in place of pins when positioning pockets or zippers.

Bodkin

This tweezer-like notion has special teeth used to draw lace, elastic, or ribbon through a casing. You can also use it for weaving.

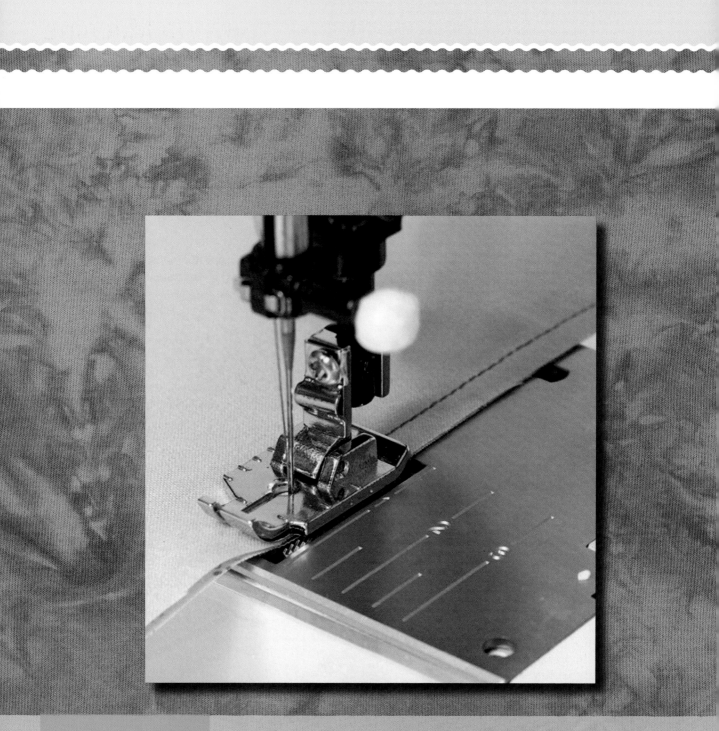

CHAPTER 2

A sewing machine equals power – power to control the destiny of your wardrobe and your home décor, power to create in any color pattern you desire, power to go against the grain and express your individuality. And in order to harness this power, you must choose to conquer your fears and tame this wild beast.

Machines

Selecting a Sewing Machine

As with any major purchase, you want to do it right the first time and get the best value for your money. Shopping for a sewing machine may seem overwhelming at times. Research your options and compare different brands. Ask yourself the following questions to determine your sewing needs before entering a store .

- **What kind of sewing interests you?** Will you make clothing for yourself, your family, and friends? Will you focus on home décor items such as pillows and curtains? Will you make crafts? Will you make gifts for holidays and special occasions? Will you only use the machine once a year to sew Halloween costumes? Will you use it for mending, hemming, or altering ready-made items? Knowing what kind of sewing interests you will help you identify which features are important.
- **What features do you want?** Are you interested in decorative stitches? Do you want a portable machine that you can take to classes? Consider which features best meet your sewing needs. Talk to your dealer and try out several different machines.
- **What kind of support do the dealer and manufacturer offer?** Does the machine come with a workbook or a video that explains how to use it? Does the dealer offer classes? Is there someone you can call with questions? Is service available? What sort of warranty does the manufacturer offer on the machine?
- **How much money can you spend?** You'll find machines priced from a few hundred dollars to several thousand dollars.

After carefully considering these questions, it's time to take a test drive. Ask your friends, family members, and co-workers to recommend a dependable sewing machine dealer. It's important to purchase a machine from a reliable dealer, as they will offer support, classes, and continued assistance with the machine.

Compare the features of several brands before purchasing. Sew on different types of fabrics, not just 100% cotton. Look for uniform and well-balanced stitches. They should not only look good, but also be consistent.

Nugget of Inspiration

Buying a sewing machine is much like buying a car. Think about what you want, do your research, and then take some machines for a test drive. Bring in fabric swatches to see how each machine performs on different types of fabrics such as woven cotton, sheer organza, denim, knit, and polyester fleece.

Sewing Machine Medley

Sewing machines are almost as varied as the people who use them. You can spend a few hundred dollars for a basic machine or invest thousands of dollars in top-of-the-line equipment and accessories. Sewing machines can be electronic or computerized. They range in the number of features as well as in price.

Electronic machines are less expensive than computerized machines and are suitable for beginner sewers. They generally come with the basic necessities such as straight and zigzag stitching and may have some features such as buttonholes and stitch pattern selection. These machines usually don't include many features.

Computerized machines come with many options such as ways to customize embroidery stitches or designs. A screen on the machine shows what you've selected. Specific machines differ but generally computerized machines offer the most features.

Motivating Memo You can sew virtually any project using the most basic sewing machine, but you may need more time and skill than you would with a machine that offers more features. For example, you can make buttonholes on a basic machine, but using a machine with a buttonhole feature greatly simplifies the task. If you have a basic machine, you must sew some types of stitches (such as decorative embroidery stitches) by hand. It's best to buy the most versatile machine you can afford.

Sewing Machines

Anatomy of a Sewing Machine

Every sewing machine has the basic components listed below. Keep in mind that each machine will look a little different and the parts may not be located in the same place. Familiarize yourself with these terms as part of your research.

- The **power switch** turns the machine on and off.
- The **presser foot** holds the fabric in place during sewing. Always lower the presser foot when sewing and lift it to remove fabric when you're finished sewing.
- The **throat plate** is a metal piece on the base (bed) of the machine under the presser foot. It has openings for the feed dogs and the needle.

Motivating Memo Some sewing machines include two types of throat plates: a zigzag and a straight stitch plate.

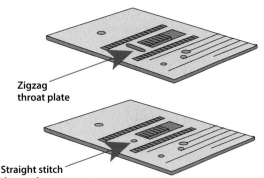

Zigzag throat plate

Straight stitch throat plate

The zigzag throat plate has a wide opening for the needle. This allows room for the needle to move from side to side. Always use this plate when zigzag stitching. The straight stitch throat plate has a small round hole for the needle. Use it when you stitch on lightweight fabrics to prevent puckering and skipped stitches. Do not use this plate for zigzagging, as the needle will break.

- The **needle** moves up and down through the fabric to form a stitch. The larger the size of a sewing machine needle, the thicker it is. Use a size 70 or 80 needle for sewing most cottons and blends.

Motivating Memo It's a good idea to insert a new needle each time you begin a new project. Your stitching will look better and you'll have less chance of snagging your fabric or having skipped stitches.

- The **feed dogs** hold the fabric tight against the presser foot as stitches are formed. Feed dogs move back and forth to "feed" (or advance) the fabric through the machine.

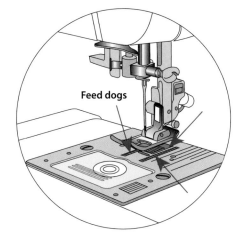

Feed dogs

- The **thread take-up** moves up and down with the needle, taking up thread slack with each stitch. Always have this lever at its highest point when you stop sewing to prevent the thread from pulling out of the needle when you start sewing.
- The **upper tension regulator** controls the tightness (tension) of the upper thread. On some machines, it may be a dial; on others it may be a disk. See your owner's manual for settings.
- **Thread guides** hold the thread as it moves from spool to needle. The number and location of guides varies with different machines. Check your owner's manual to see where they are located on your machine.
- The **spool pin** holds the spool of thread.
- The **bobbin winder** holds the bobbin while thread winds from the spool onto the bobbin.
- The **balance wheel** (also called the handwheel or flywheel) makes a complete turn with each stitch. You can use this wheel to move the needle up and down by hand without using the motor.
- The **stitch length regulator** determines how long each stitch will be.

   Use 10 to 12 stitches per inch (3 to 2.5mm stitch length) for sewing most seams.

   Use 6 to 8 stitches per inch (4 to 3.25mm stitch length) for basting. Basting is a longer stitch that temporarily holds two edges together.

- The **stitch width regulator** determines how wide a zigzag stitch will be.
- The **bobbin** holds the lower thread.
- The **foot control** determines how fast or slow the machine sews, much like the gas pedal on a car.

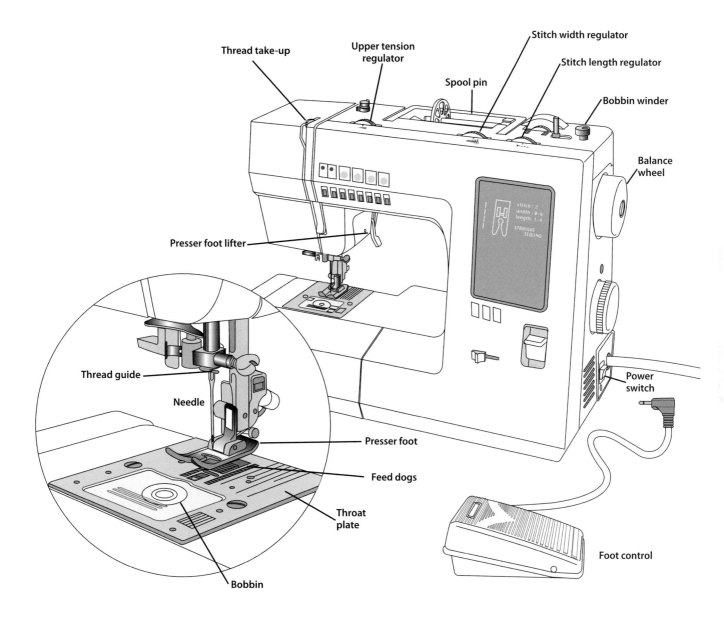

Thread take-up

Upper tension regulator

Stitch width regulator

Stitch length regulator

Spool pin

Bobbin winder

Balance wheel

Presser foot lifter

stitch : 2
width : 0-6
length : 1-4
STRAIGHT
SEWING

Power switch

Thread guide

Needle

Presser foot

Feed dogs

Throat plate

Foot control

Bobbin

Features

The following are some sewing machine features that are not necessarily on every machine. Determine which ones are the most important to the type of sewing you'll be doing. When applicable, test the features as you compare different machines.

- **Free arm**. Does the machine convert from a flat sewing area (flat bed) to a more open sewing area (free arm)? A free arm is good for sewing tubes such as sleeves and pant legs.
- **Cabinet or portable**. How much room do you have for a sewing machine? A cabinet machine is like furniture. A portable can easily be moved around the house as well as taken to classes.
- **Stitches**. How many stitches are programmed into the machine? This can vary from as few as five to as many as hundreds. Stitches fall into two categories: utility and decorative. Utility stitches are the straight stitch, zigzag (in several widths), blind hem, and stretch. Decorative stitches range from abstract shapes to objects such as hearts, flowers, and leaves. Generally, the more decorative stitches a machine has, the higher the price.
- **Built-in needle threader**. Is this feature easy to use? Does it work consistently?
- **Buttonhole procedure**. Does the machine stitch even, neat buttonholes? Is the feature easy to use?
- **Bobbin winder**. Is it easy to wind the bobbin? Does the machine stop winding when the bobbin is full?
- **Automatic tension**. Does the machine set the thread tension automatically? If not, is it easy to adjust the tension and achieve a balanced stitch?
- **Adjustable needle positions**. Can you move the needles to accommodate different feet and types of stitches? This is especially helpful when topstitching and inserting zippers.

Using the Manual

Your owner's manual is a great resource for learning how to thread and adjust the machine, plus how to wind and thread the bobbin. Each manufacturer has its own techniques/instructions for these basic tasks. Your manual also offers troubleshooting tips to help if you have problems with stitches or the machine's operation.

Most manuals contain a list of accessories available from the manufacturer, such as special presser feet, cleaning equipment, and replacement parts.

Nugget of Inspiration

Personalize your owner's manual by putting sticky notes on pages you refer to often. It's amazing how many times you'll go back to certain pages; the markers really speed up this process.

Maintenance

Sewing machines are sturdy pieces of equipment, so a little regular maintenance goes a long way toward keeping your machine in good working order. Cleaning your machine before each project reduces the likelihood of mechanical problems while you're sewing.

Check your manual for specific guidelines on maintaining your machine.

- Insert a new needle for each project. Don't wait for a needle to break or start snagging your fabric. A worn needle can develop tiny burrs and other imperfections that will cause your machine to skip stitches or make uneven stitches.
- Whenever you change the top thread, "floss" your machine by clipping the thread at the spool and pulling the thread out through the needle. This helps remove built-up lint.

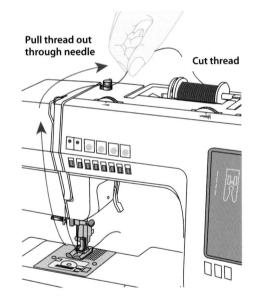

Pull thread out through needle

Cut thread

- Dust or wipe out the bobbin area to remove lint. Refer to the owner's manual and, if it's recommended, place a drop of oil where indicated.

Dust out bobbin area to remove lint

Threading

Check your instruction manual to learn how to thread your machine and wind your bobbin. Use the same kind of thread in both places. Practice until you're comfortable winding a bobbin and threading the machine.

1 Wind the bobbin.

2 Insert the bobbin. If your machine has a front-loading bobbin, put the bobbin in its case. If your machine has a drop-in bobbin, insert the bobbin.

3 Thread the top of the machine.

4 Bring up the bobbin thread to get the machine ready for sewing.

   a. Hold the needle thread in your left hand.

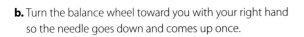

   b. Turn the balance wheel toward you with your right hand so the needle goes down and comes up once.

   c. Gently pull the thread in your left hand to pull up a loop. This loop is the bobbin thread.

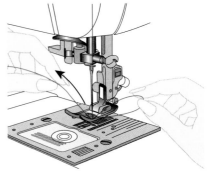

   d. Grasp both threads and bring them under the presser foot to the back of the machine.

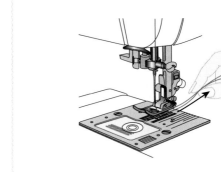

Motivating Memo Bobbins are inexpensive, so keep extras on hand. Before you start a big project, wind two or more bobbins so you don't have to stop in the middle of a seam, unthread your machine, and wind a fresh bobbin.

Presser Feet

The right presser foot can save you time and increase your creativity. Even though you'll use a standard all-purpose presser foot and a straight or zigzag stitch for most sewing projects, the accessory box that comes with your sewing machine contains an array of presser feet.

Note: Your presser feet may not look exactly like the ones pictured. Look for a foot that has similar characteristics. Start experimenting today – you'll discover new sewing shortcuts and expand your creative horizons.

- **Standard or general purpose** feet are mostly used for everyday sewing. The wide opening is proportionate to the width of your machine's zigzag stitch (from 4 to 9mm or ⅛" to ¼", depending on the sewing machine). This foot is sometimes called a zigzag foot. Your machine's throat plate has an opening of similar size so the needle can easily enter the bobbin area to form a perfect stitch.

- The **blind hem** foot is one of the most versatile feet in your accessory box. It is traditionally used for hemming woven and knit fabrics. You can also use it to apply patch pockets and appliqués, and it makes straight edgestitching a breeze! Move the adjustable guide closer to or farther from the left side of the foot to accommodate fabrics of various weights and textures.

- The **buttonhole** foot moves forward and backward in a sliding tray attached to the machine, making it easy for you to sew identical buttonholes with smooth, uniform stitching. Markings along one or both sides of the foot indicate the buttonhole length.

- **Patchwork or quilting** feet are mostly used for accurate piecing in quilting. The right edge of the patchwork foot is precisely ¼" from the center needle position, providing an accurate guide for making a ¼" seam allowance.

- The **open toe** foot lets you see more of the area around the needle when sewing decorative stitches or when satin stitching around appliqués. The toe area may be completely open, or its center may be clear plastic. This makes it easy to see stitches as they form on fabric. The underside has a hollowed or grooved section that lets dense stitching move smoothly under the foot without bunching beneath the needle.

- A **roller** foot easily feeds finicky fabrics. A metal roller leaves no imprint on fabrics. The roller foot is great for sewing on napped or slippery fabrics like silk, leather, velvet, vinyl, velveteen, and corduroy.

- **Zipper** feet are specially shaped to allow you to sew closer to the zipper teeth.

- The **button/fringe** foot is used to sew on buttons. Some machine manufacturers may refer to this as a fringe foot.

Standard

Blind hem

Buttonhole

Quilting

Open toe

Roller

Zipper

Button/fringe

Stitches

Straight Stitch

- The straight stitch is the basic, most used stitch for general sewing.
- Use it for almost all seams, gathering, darts, pleats, etc.

Zigzag Stitch

- The zigzag stitch is a common stitch used to finish seam edges and apply appliqués.

Multi-Zigzag Stitch

- The multi-zigzag is a variation of the zigzag stitch formed by three stitches in each direction.
- It is often used when a stretch stitch or understitching is recommended.

Blind Hem Stitch

- The blind hem stitch sews several straight stitches, then zigzags once to the left.
- It is often used for stitching hems. When a hem is folded, the tip of the zigzag catches a few threads of the project fabric for a tiny hem stitch.

Decorative Stitch

- These are stitch patterns used for decoration.
- The patterns can be abstract or objects such as flowers, leaves, stars, hearts, scallops, etc.

Nugget of Inspiration

Make a test sample of all the programmed stitches in your machine. Stitch each one on a piece of fabric, label it by stitch number, and store the sample with your machine manual. You'll get to see what each one looks like stitched out, and have a handy reference for the future.

Straight stitch

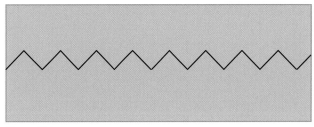

Zigzag stitch

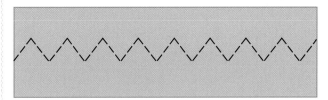

Multi-zigzag stitch

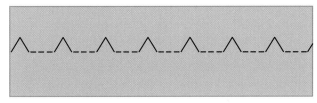

Blind hem stitch

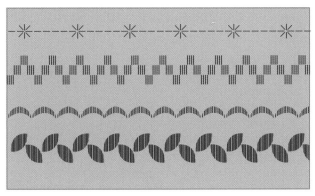

Decorative stitches

Practice Makes Perfect

Now that you are more familiar with your machine, take some time to practice using it before stitching on your first project. As you gain experience, you will learn to control the speed of the machine and your stitching will get straighter.

1 Remove the thread from your machine.

2 Practice stitching on a piece of paper.

Motivating Memo You probably won't be sewing on paper but this exercise lets you see exactly where you're stitching so you can practice sewing straighter.

- Draw some straight lines (or use a sheet of notebook paper). Guide the machine along those lines as you stitch.
- The largest portion of the paper should be to the left of the presser foot.
- Lower the presser foot using the presser foot lifter.
- Turn the balance wheel toward you by hand as you gently press on the foot control to help get the machine started.

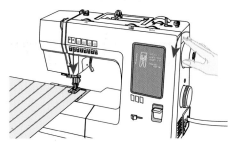

- As the machine begins to stitch, remove your hand from the wheel and place it to the right of the needle. Place your left hand to the left of the needle. Use your hands to guide the paper through the machine. Don't push or pull the paper; just guide it so the stitching follows the line.
- To stop, release the pressure on the foot control. Turn the balance wheel by hand until the thread take-up is as high as it will go. (Some machines do this automatically.)

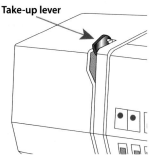

Take-up lever

- Practice until you can put the right amount of pressure on the foot control so the machine runs smoothly at a medium speed (without jerks) and you follow the marked lines.
- Most machines have a control for stitching in reverse. Check your instruction manual to see how to stitch in reverse on your machine. Practice stitching backward and forward.

3 Draw some curved lines with both inside and outside curves. Practice stitching along those lines until you can guide the paper easily and run the machine smoothly. If you stitch slowly, it's easier to follow the curves.

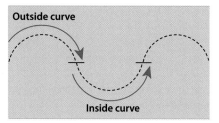

Outside curve

Inside curve

4 Draw some corners and practice turning while stitching. This is called pivoting.

- Stitch to the corner. Stop with the needle down in the paper. Lift the presser foot.

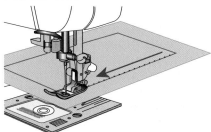

- Turn the paper so the foot lines up with the next stitching line.
- Lower the presser foot and continue stitching.

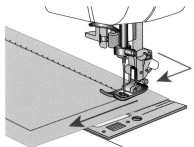

- Practice until it's easy to turn corners.

Nugget of Inspiration

Stitch designs on paper to create unique greeting cards. Draw a design on colored paper and stitch. Back the stitched area with another color paper and create the card. Use the cards as invitations, thank you notes, or just for dropping someone a note.

Anatomy of a Serger

A serger gives you the power to speed your sewing and make it much easier. Simply stated, a serger stitches a seam, trims off the excess fabric, and finishes the raw edges all at the same time – at a speed nearly twice that of a conventional machine!

A serger uses three, four, five, or as many as eight threads instead of the two threads used on a conventional sewing machine. Because of those extra threads, a serger looks more complicated than a conventional sewing machine. Read on for tips to help you tame the wild beast – making threading and stitching with a serger fast and easy.

A serger will not replace your sewing machine. Rather it can complement a conventional machine to enhance speed, neatness, and creativity.

- The **stitch finger** can be located on the throat plate or on the presser foot. It is a metal prong that stays between the fabric and the thread as the serged stitch is formed.
- A serger may have one or two **needles**. One needle or both can be used, depending on the type of stitch desired.
- A serger has two **blades** – a stationary blade and a second blade that moves up and down in synchronization with the needle(s). Working together in a jaw-like configuration, the blades "bite" the fabric as you stitch, trimming the seam allowances to ¼".

Nugget of Inspiration

Because sergers go very fast, it's tempting to zip along at a breakneck pace. However, keep in mind that when the blades cut the fabric, it is permanent. It is surprisingly easy to get caught up in the moment, enjoying the feel of the fabric as it whooshes through your fingers. But sometimes extra fabric sneaks under the blades and suddenly you're left with a big mess! If this should happen, mend the hole as best as you can. Then have a good laugh at yourself and continue with your project.

- Instead of a bobbin, sergers have two **loopers** that work together, similar to knitting needles. The **lower looper** uses the last thread on the right. It doesn't stitch through the fabric, but passes under the fabric. It interlocks with the upper looper and is secured by the needle thread. The **upper looper** uses the second thread from the right. It also doesn't stitch through the fabric. It passes over the fabric, interlocks with the lower looper, and is secured by the needle thread.
- Sergers have teeth-like grippers called **feed dogs** nestled in the throat plate. Feed dogs on a serger are nearly twice as long as feed dogs on a sewing machine.
- The extra long **presser foot** seldom needs to be raised when beginning to serge. Simply lay the fabric on the bed of the machine and begin to sew; the fabric will be evenly fed under the foot.

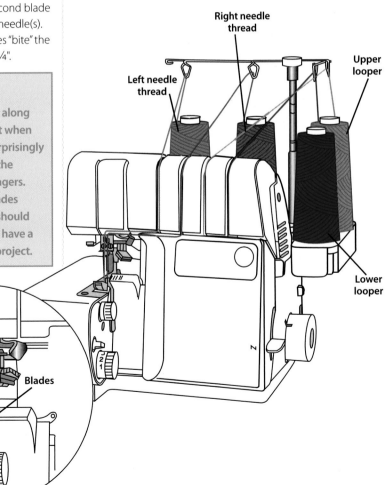

Right needle thread

Upper looper

Left needle thread

Lower looper

Needles

Blades

Presser foot

Feed dogs

Maintenance

Perform routine maintenance on your serger before you begin each project to minimize operating problems.

- Brush out the area around the feed dogs. This is even more important on a serger than on a sewing machine because the serger trims fabric, causing lint to accumulate quickly. This can jam the machine and reduce stitch quality.
- Check the thread path or threading sequence. Incorrect threading is a common problem, so it's a good idea to check each step.

> ### Nugget of Inspiration
> Many a seasoned seamstress has shed more than a few tears while trying to thread a serger. If you're one of the lucky ones with a Jet-Air Threading serger, you might not have experienced this dilemma. For the rest of us, the thing to remember about sergers is this: Learning how to thread it is the first step to empowerment.

- Check the needles. If your serger uses regular sewing machine needles, change the needles with each project. If the serger uses industrial needles, plan to change needles every two to three projects. If a needle is worn, damaged, or causes skipped stitches, replace it immediately, no matter how long it's been there.

Threading Sequence

When threading a serger, it's important to follow the correct threading sequence. Otherwise, your threading efforts will be in vain. If you thread the machine in the wrong order, it will not work. This is true for all sergers that do not have Jet-Air Threading. Always thread the loopers before threading the needle. Check your serger manual to see which looper to thread first and for precise recommendations for your machine.

Serger Thread

Serger thread is made of two strands (ply) twisted together, while thread made for a conventional sewing machine is made of three strands. Three or four threads are joined to form each serged seam. The lighter weight two-ply thread keeps the serged seam from becoming too bulky.

Serger thread is spiral wound on cones, while sewing machine thread is parallel wound on spools.

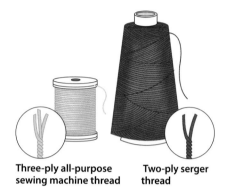

Three-ply all-purpose sewing machine thread   **Two-ply serger thread**

Parallel wound thread can be used on a serger if a special spool cap is placed over the spool to keep the thread from catching on the rim of the spool.

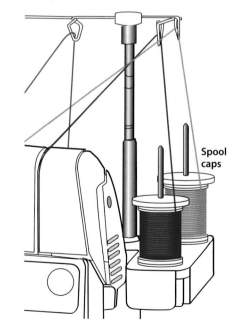

Spool caps

Motivating Memo Use all-purpose serger thread while you are learning to serge. Many types of decorative threads can also be used on a serger. After you become more experienced, try using some of these threads for special effects.

Overlock Stitch

Although a serger can make several types of stitches, the stitch used for most serging is called an overlock. Check your instruction manual to be sure your serger is adjusted for an overlock stitch.

You need a 2" thread chain behind the presser foot before you begin serging. Make this chain by following the instructions below.

1 Holding the looper and needle threads with your left hand, lower the presser foot.

2 Turn the wheel with your right hand as you lightly press the foot control. This helps get the machine started.

3 Continue pressing the foot control as the thread chain forms.

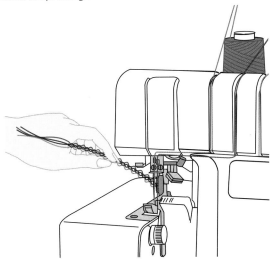

Begin stitching to form thread chain

Before stitching on a project, always test the serger tension on a scrap of the fabric. Refer to your instruction manual if the stitch is not balanced or if the fabric puckers.

A serged seam is generally ¼" to ⅜" wide. You must position your fabric in the serger so the seam is sewn at that position.

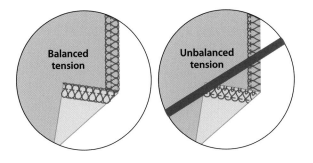

Seam Finishing

Fabric that ravels needs a seam finish to prevent fraying, especially if the finished garment will be machine-laundered. Serging is a quick and easy method to finish seams. Use a 3 thread or 3/4 thread overlock stitch to finish seams.

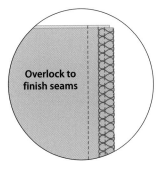

Overlock to finish seams

CHAPTER 3
Fabrics

Fabric cannot judge us or reject us. Fabric cannot see our imperfections and faults. Fabric embraces us for who we are, accepting and celebrating our differences. Fabric allows us to express ourselves, to play out our fantasies, and capture our dreams.

In sewing, as in life, it's important to know right from wrong.

Learn the correct terms for working with fabric and it will eliminate confusion when following instructions for cutting and sewing.

- The **right side** is the side of the fabric that shows on the outside. With printed fabrics, the design is printed on the right side. With napped fabrics, the nap is pronounced on the right side.
- The **wrong side** is the side of the fabric that doesn't show; it faces the inside. On printed fabrics, the unprinted side is the wrong side. On napped fabrics, the nap is less pronounced on the wrong side.
- The **selvages** are the tightly woven finished edges of the fabric. Selvages do not ravel.
- Yarns on the **lengthwise grain** of the fabric run the same direction as the selvage (parallel to it). Lengthwise yarns are usually stronger than crosswise yarns. Most projects are cut with the lengthwise yarns going up and down.
- Yarns on the **crosswise grain** run across the fabric from one selvage to the other (perpendicular to the selvage). Most projects are cut with the crosswise grain going around.

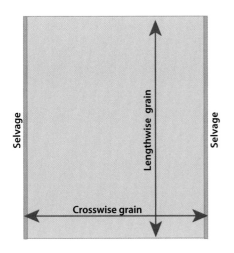

- The **bias** is an imaginary diagonal line between the lengthwise and crosswise threads on a fabric. True bias lies at a 45° angle to the selvage and has more stretch than lengthwise or crosswise grains.

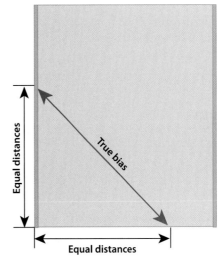

- The **nap** is the pile and/or hair on fabrics that have a definite up and down. Napped fabrics include corduroy, velvet, camel's hair, mohair, brushed denim, and sweatshirt fleece.
- **One-way designs** have a definite top and bottom printed on fabric.

An example of one-way design on a fabric.

Nugget of Inspiration

Be careful not to be too literal when learning new fabric vocabulary words. For example, contrary to what you might initially think, fabric nap is not an instruction to lie down with your fabric and catch some shuteye!

Fiber Content

Fibers are the materials used to manufacture fabric. A fiber looks like a fine thread. Some fibers occur naturally; others are manmade. To make manmade fibers, special liquids are forced through tiny holes and hardened to form continuous threads.

- **Natural fibers** include cotton, flax, silk, and wool. These fibers have been used for centuries and come from the following sources:
  - cotton from the boll of a cotton plant.
  - flax from the stalk of the flax plant. Flax is used to make linen fabric.
  - silk from cocoons spun by silkworms.
  - wool from the fleece of animals such as sheep, goats, alpacas, and camels.

- **Manmade fibers** are usually made from chemical solutions containing products made from oil. Some common manmade fibers are nylon, acrylic, and polyester. Rayon is a manmade fiber produced by adding chemicals to a natural cellulose such as wood.
- **Fabric blends** are made by combining two or more different fibers. For example, a fabric may be a blend of 50% polyester and 50% cotton, or a blend of 75% rayon and 25% cotton. Combining several kinds of fibers to make a fabric gives the finished fabric some of the characteristics of each of those fibers.

Fabric Construction

Fabrics are made in three ways: woven, knit, and nonwoven. Learn to recognize all three.

- In **woven** fabric the yarns go over and under one another. Examples include denim, corduroy, broadcloth, batiste, organza, challis, wool coating, silk, satin, and velvet.

- In **nonwoven fabrics** heat, moisture, and pressure are applied to fibers, forcing them close together. Sometimes chemicals are added to hold the fibers together. Examples include many interfacings, polyester fleece, and felt.

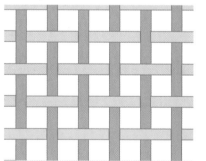

Woven fabric

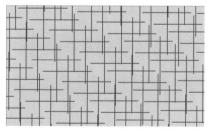

Nonwoven fabric

- In **knits** one loop of yarn is pulled through another loop. Most knits stretch. Examples include interlock, sweatshirt fleece, and sweater knits.

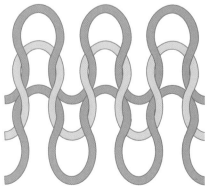

Knit fabric

Fabric Selection

It's important to choose fabric carefully. If you select the wrong fabric, your project may not look, fit, or drape as you want it to.

1 Refer to the list of suggested fabrics on the back of the pattern envelope to see what kinds of fabrics are recommended. Specific fabrics are suited for each pattern. Sometimes a pattern will also list fabrics that should *not* be used for that pattern.

> SUGGESTED FABRICS: All Garments • Cotton • Cotton Blends • Chambray • Challis • Rip-stop Nylon • Supplex • NOTE: All Garments-Not Suitable for Diagonals.

2 Look at the fabric. Check whether the fabric is straight.
- Check that the ends of the fabric are square. Line up the ends of the folded fabric with the corner of a counter or table. Both ends should be even and straight with the corner.
- If the fabric's cut edges are not straight, you may need to purchase extra fabric.

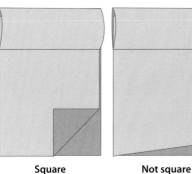

Square **Not square**

3 Check the fabric's design.
- If the fabric has a printed design arranged in definite rows, be sure the design is printed straight, both across and up and down the fabric.
- If the design is not straight, you may want to look for another fabric.
- For your first projects, don't choose striped or plaid fabric. These designs must be matched at the seamlines. Save such fabrics until you have more experience.

4 Read the important information on the end of the fabric bolt. It tells you:
- fiber content
- fabric width
- cost
- care instructions. Does the fabric need to be dry cleaned? Can it be machine washed? Will it need ironing? When you purchase fabric, make a note of this information.

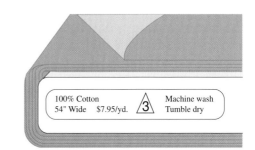

| 100% Cotton | | Machine wash |
| 54" Wide $7.95/yd. | /3\ | Tumble dry |

Nugget of Inspiration

Create your own care labels to insert into your projects. Create the labels on your computer and print them onto photo transfer paper. Or write the instructions on a label with a permanent fabric pen.

Motivating Memo If your fabric is washable, always prewash the fabric after you purchase it. This makes the fabric easier to sew. Wash and dry the fabric according to the care instructions on the bolt before cutting out your garment. After your fabric has been prewashed, clip off a small triangle at one corner. Then you can later tell at a glance that your fabric is ready for the sewing machine. Plus, if the fabric shrinks, the shrinking will happen before you sew your project.

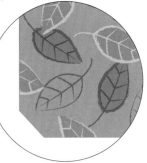

Clip off corner

5 If your pattern calls for interfacing, purchase it at the same time you purchase your fabric so you have it when you need it. The amount of interfacing needed is listed on the yardage chart on the back of the pattern envelope under each pattern view. (For more information on interfacing, see page 37.)

6 Purchase the notions (zippers, buttons, hooks and eyes, thread) needed for your project at the same time you buy your fabric. Check the list on the back of the pattern envelope.

Specialty Fabrics

What makes these fabrics special? Well, they're definitely unique and don't fit neatly into categories. Some of the fabric listed below you may have never thought of as fabric. Whether you want to make Halloween costumes, lunch bags, or activity projects for children, you'll find a huge variety of fabrics that can help you reach your goal.

Because these fabrics are so unique, a basic pattern or project is perfect for them. For example, a lunch bag made from oilcloth or vinyl fabric is a great project for a beginner.

Oilcloth

For a vintage look, try using oilcloth. Colorful and fun, it's perfect for lunch bags, totes, tablecloths, aprons, and more. Constructed of vinyl film on cotton mesh, it's water, stain, and soil resistant. To clean it, simply wipe with a warm soapy sponge. Do not machine wash.

Sensible Sewing Tips

- Keep a hot iron away from the surface of oilcloth because it could melt the oilcloth fabric surface. If needed, use a warm, dry iron on the wrong side of the fabric with a damp press cloth. Do not use steam and don't hold the iron down in one place very long. Or use a wooden presser like the Little Wooden Iron to press the oilcloth.
- Use the standard sewing machine presser foot or a Teflon foot. A smooth Teflon-coated foot glides over hard-to-sew fabrics like oilcloth, preventing the fabric from tugging and pulling against the foot. If you don't have a Teflon foot, use tissue paper or wax paper between the oilcloth and the presser foot. The paper will help the fabric glide smoothly and the stitching perforates the paper, making it easy to remove. After sewing, tear the paper away.
- Use a size 80 universal needle.
- Thread the top and bobbin of the machine with coordinating all-purpose thread.
- Pin marks are permanent in oilcloth, so binding and hem clips are good substitutes. They firmly hold the edges in place, yet leave no marks on the fabric when they're removed.
- Since oilcloth doesn't ravel, finish the edges with decorative shears such as scallop shears, pinking shears, or a wavy blade rotary cutter.

Make your lunch, then carry it in a colorful reusable oilcloth lunch bag. It's easy to sew, and even easier to clean.

Vinyl

Although it's not usually thought of as fabric, vinyl is easy to incorporate into sewing projects. Different types of vinyl include clear, reinforced, and traditional. Vinyl is easy to clean – you simply wipe it with a damp cloth. This versatile "fabric" doesn't fray, has no grain, and is waterproof. It's ideal for crafts, home dec projects, and so much more.

Sensible Sewing Tips

• Follow the guidelines detailed for oilcloth with the following exception: Adjust your machine for a longer stitch (3.5mm). Smaller stitches weaken the fabric.

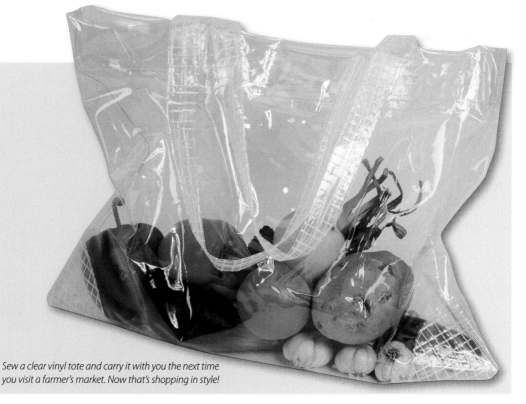

Sew a clear vinyl tote and carry it with you the next time you visit a farmer's market. Now that's shopping in style!

Chalkboard Fabric

As the name implies, this fabric functions like a chalkboard – write on it with chalk and wipe it clean with a sponge. The fabric is available in black and green, just like real chalkboards. Durable and easy to sew, this unique fabric is great for creating calendars, memo boards, and children's activity projects. Or just cover surfaces and let the kids go to town! Machine washing is not recommended.

Sensible Sewing Tips

• You can handle chalkboard fabric the same as oilcloth except that you'll need to cure it before using it for the first time.

❶ Place the fabric on a flat surface.

❷ Lay a piece of chalk on its side on the fabric surface and rub the chalk all over the fabric, side to side and top to bottom.

❸ Clean the fabric with a damp sponge, then repeat the process. The chalkboard fabric is now cured and ready for use.

If you're constantly on the go, keep track of appointments, meetings, and upcoming events by sewing an attractive chalkboard fabric memo board. Updating it is as easy as getting out a piece of chalk.

Iron Quick

This unique fabric reflects heat and resists burning, making it ideal for oven mitts, hot pads, casserole carriers, and ironing board covers. Iron Quick is available in two versions: regular and quilted. Washable and air dryable, this sturdy fabric is ideal for creating all kinds of kitchen accessories.

Sensible Sewing Tips

- When working with quilted Iron Quick fabric, mark the outlines of each section you're cutting out on the Iron Quick. Before you cut out the sections, place a drop or two of seam sealant (see page 58) where each quilted stitching line meets the traced outline. Allow the seam sealant to dry, then cut out the sections. This helps secure the quilted stitching lines and eliminates unsightly loose thread ends when you're finished.
- Use a size 80 universal needle to sew Iron Quick.
- Position the Iron Quick so the aluminized surface faces the heat.

Make potholders for every season by adding easy-sew Iron Quick Fabric to layers of your favorite seasonal fabrics and batting. Bind the edges, and you're finished. It's all simple straight stitching.

Napped or Pile Fabric

Napped fabrics include camel's hair, mohair, brushed denim, and sweatshirt fleece. Pile fabrics include chenille, corduroy, fake fur, fleece, terry, and velvet.

When you pet a cat or dog the wrong way, you'll notice that its fur stands on end and may appear to be a different color. Napped and pile fabrics are similar. Because of the way they're constructed, these fabrics reflect light differently from different positions, so you must cut all pattern pieces with the tops facing in the same direction. You usually need more fabric to accommodate this special layout. Patterns that suggest napped or pile fabrics usually provide napped layout diagrams and extra yardage requirements.

Sensible Sewing Tips
- Take special care when pressing napped or pile fabrics. Use a press cloth and press from the wrong side. Test the heat, the amount of steam, and the pressure on scraps before pressing your project.
- Stitch in the direction of the nap or pile.
- Use a size 90, 100, or 110 denim/sharp needle for napped fabrics.
- Use a size 80 universal needle for fleece.
- Use a size 90 stretch needle for fur.
- Use a size 70 or 80 universal needle for velvet.
- Use a denim/sharp needle for corduroy.

Select fabrics and colorations that suit your style and décor, then stitch basic fabric rectangles into one-of-a-kind pillows.

Sheer Fabric

Fabrics classified as sheers include organdy, organza, handkerchief linen, batiste, rayon challis, mesh, crochet-type knits, net, lace, chiffon, gauze, and tulle.

Sheer or transparent fabrics vary widely in weight and type. Use these fabrics in a variety of projects such as gift bags, bridal wear, curtains, eveningwear, costumes, linens, and much more.

When you first start working with these fabrics, stick to basic projects until you get the hang of sewing on them. They can be tricky to sew, but don't let that deter you from incorporating them into your projects. Just go slow and be careful, and soon you'll be sewing sheer fabrics like a pro.

Sensible Sewing Tips

- Use silk pins or fine needles to pin sheer fabrics because they snag easily and ravel badly. They're susceptible to marring by pins, needles, and even rough hands.
- Sheer fabrics don't ease well, so choose a pattern with little easing at sleeves and seams.
- To prevent seams from puckering, hold the fabric taut as it feeds through the machine.
- Use a size 60 universal needle for organza.
- Use a size 70 or 80 universal needle for linen.

Your gift will do double duty when you wrap it in a fabric gift bag. The sewing is easy, and the recipient will long remember both the gift and its reusable package.

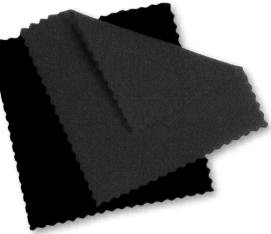

High Loft Fleece

This lightweight, high loft 100% polyester knit offers warmth without weight. It is popular for outerwear because it doesn't readily absorb moisture. Like many knits, fleece is usually 60" wide. It has a lot of crosswise stretch, while the lengthwise grain is relatively stable.

Sensible Sewing Tips

- To identify the right side of high loft fleece fabric, pull on the crosswise grain. The fleece curls to the wrong side.
- Use a size 90 stretch or size 80 universal needle.
- Use a longer stitch length, 3.0 mm.
- Seam finishes are unnecessary because fleece doesn't ravel.
- Finger press fleece; using an iron flattens the nap.

Transform high loft fleece into unique pillows for every room in your house. Because fleece doesn't ravel, a few snips of the scissors and straight stitching are all you need to create interesting accents.

Craft/Costume Fabric

Costume and craft patterns may recommend that you use anything from silk lamé to fake fur. Treat these fabrics like you would any other; pay attention to the care instructions and don't be intimidated by their unique features.

Sensible Sewing Tips

• Never press on the right side of fake fur. On long-hair furs, finger press only.
• To cut fake fur, first mark the pattern outline on the wrong side of the fabric, then cut carefully through **only the fabric backing**, using the point of a shears. Separate the fur as you cut to avoid cutting through the pile.
• When sewing fake fur, lengthen the stitches to eight to 10 stitches per inch, approximately a 3.5 setting.

From elegant lame to fake fur, specialty fabrics present limitless opportunities for sewing everything from handbags to costumes.

Nugget of Inspiration

If you're attracted to really unique fabrics and like using them in unconventional ways, visit fabric stores around Halloween time. You'll find a wide variety of fabrics like fake fur, animal skin, sequined fabrics, and other unexpected treasures. Stock up on these fabrics and experiment by using them for home dec projects such as pillows, curtains, or lampshades. It's a fun and easy way to add some pizzazz to your decorating scheme!

Felt

Felt is a nonwoven fabric usually made from wool, acrylic, or a fiber blend. It has no bias, no grain, and no right or wrong side. Felt is made by using moisture, heat, and pressure to bond loose fibers together, then pounding them to force fibers closer together.

Felt is easy to sew. It doesn't ravel or fray so you don't have to finish the edges. However, it does tend to bag at stress points such as knees, elbows, and seat, and is difficult to mend.

Sensible Sewing Tips
- Use a size 80 or 90 universal needle.
- Lengthen stitches to eight to 10 stitches per inch, approximately a 3.5 setting.

Motivating Memo Prewashing wool felt causes as much as 75% shrinkage. You'll need to buy extra felt if you're going to prewash it before starting your project. (Prewashing may eliminate the need to dry clean your finished project.)

Synthetic Suede

Synthetic suede has the luxurious look and drape, soft feel, and tough durability of natural suede, yet offers sew-ability, stain and soil resistance, and easy care. This fabric is completely machine washable and dryable, and wrinkle resistant. Because suede doesn't ravel, edges can be easily finished with a scallop shears or rotary cutter. Its stain and abrasion resistance makes synthetic suede practical for a variety of items such as purses and pillows. The internal "scrim" allows the fabric to breathe and to remain strong and supple.

Sensible Sewing Tips
- Use a size 80 microtex sharp needle.
- Use a Teflon foot, which will glide over fabrics such as synthetic suede, preventing the fabric from tugging and pulling against the foot.
- Lengthen stitches to eight to 10 stitches per inch, approximately a 3.5 setting.

Interfacing

Interfacings are hidden inside garments, but they're essential for good construction. Fused to the wrong side of fabric, interfacing adds shape and body. Patterns list the amount of interfacing you need in a yardage chart on the back of the envelope. Choose an interfacing that is lighter in weight than your fabric. (See page 63 for more detailed information about interfacing.)

Weights and Types

The key to using interfacing successfully is choosing the correct weight and type for your fabric. Interfacing is available in both fusible and nonfusible types. Fusible interfacing is easier to work with, and therefore is better suited to beginning sewers. In this book, we discuss only fusible interfacing.

Care instructions for interfacing should be the same as those for your garment fabric. The weight of the interfacing should complement and reinforce the weight and shape of your garment fabric. Choose fusible interfacing one weight lighter than your fabric since the fusing resins add weight once the interfacing is fused to the fabric. For example, if using a medium weight fabric, choose a lightweight fusible interfacing. The following chart includes a few of the available interfacings.

Name/Primary Use	Weight/Fabrication	Fiber Content	Width
Knits and Wovens			
Pellon Bi-Stretch Lite	sheer woven	100% polyester	30"
Lightweight Pellon	lightweight nonwoven	70% nylon/30% polyester	22"
Whisper Weft	lightweight woven	60% polyester/40% rayon	48"
Knits			
Fusible Tricot	light/midweight knit	100% nylon	60"
Wovens			
Stacy's Shape Flex	light/midweight woven	100% cotton	22"

Storage

To store interfacing, roll it onto a tube to prevent wrinkles and save space. Tuck the interfacing instructions for fusing inside the tube.

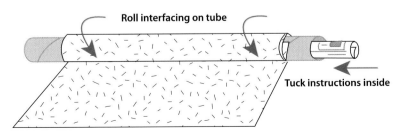

Roll interfacing on tube

Tuck instructions inside

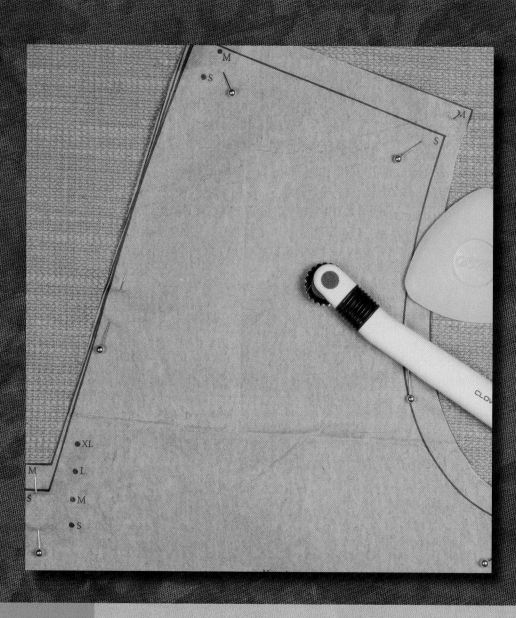

CHAPTER 4

Patterns are the road map on your sewing journey, offering quiet guidance free from criticism. To reach your goal, you must decipher the mysteries of the pattern's seemingly cryptic pieces. Within the maze of lines, markings, and letters lies the promise of exquisite creations, which emerge at the end of your journey.

Patterns

Pattern catalogs and magazines offer an enticing selection of ready-to-sew fashions, accessories, and home dec items.

Because your pattern will be the road map for your project, make the catalog area your first stop at the fabric store.

The pattern envelope offers a wealth of valuable information; study both the front and back carefully. The front shows photos or sketches (called "views") of all the style variations included in the pattern. These views usually show the project from the front.

The back of the pattern envelope gives detailed purchasing and sewing information including:

- Back views of the garments, including details such as darts, pockets, and variations in length.
- The body measurement chart, which usually gives the bust, waist, and hip measurements, along with corresponding pattern sizes.
- The suggested fabrics list, indicating which fabrics are recommended as well as fabrics that are less likely to work for this pattern style.

Motivating Memo Selecting fabric can overwhelm even experienced sewers, especially with the array of beautiful fabrics available today. Don't hesitate to ask a sales clerk for help finding the types of fabrics recommended for your pattern.

- The yardage chart, showing how much fabric and interfacing you'll need for each size and fabric width.
- The notions section, which lists the other supplies you need to complete the project such as buttons, snaps, hooks and eyes, zippers, elastic, and thread.
- The finished garment measurements show the difference between what the body measures and what the pattern measures. This tells you the amount of ease or "living" room the pattern allows.

Nugget of Inspiration

When you're at the fabric store picking out fabric, buy all the notions you need for the project. If for some reason you should decide to start sewing at midnight and you haven't purchased a zipper or thread, there's nothing you can do except wait in frustration for the store to open.

The back of the pattern envelope provides a lot of important information.

The front of the pattern envelope shows the finished garments.

Yardage

To determine the amount of fabric needed:

- Find the view you are making on the left side of the yardage chart on the pattern envelope.
- Find the line under that view that lists the width of your fabric.
- Find your pattern size at the top of the chart.
- Follow the pattern size column down until it meets the fabric width line. This is the amount of fabric you need.

	Small	Medium	Large	X-Large	XX-Large
	31-1/2—32-1/2	34—36	38—40	42—44	46—48
	33-1/2—34-1/2	36—38	40—42	44—46	48—50
Top					
45" ***	2-5/8	2-3/4	3	3-1/4	3-3/8
60" ***	1-7/8	1-7/8	1-7/8	1-7/8	2
Interfacing - 21" thru 25", 3/8 yd.					
Pants					
45" ***	2-5/8	2-5/8	2-3/4	2-3/4	2-3/4
60" ***	2	2-3/8	2-3/8	2-3/4	2-3/4

Guide Sheet

Think of the guide sheet as your instruction book. It includes:

- Illustrations of all the pattern pieces for the different views.
- Pattern markings that explain the symbols and terms used in the pattern.
- General information about interfacing, adjusting the pattern, cutting and marking, and sewing, which helps you complete the project.
- Cutting layout illustrations showing how to place the pattern pieces on the fabric before you cut them out.
- Step-by-step instructions and illustrations showing how to make the project from start to finish.

Motivating Memo Before beginning a project, it's a good idea to read through the guide sheet to get a general idea of the complete process. It's like checking the map before taking a trip.

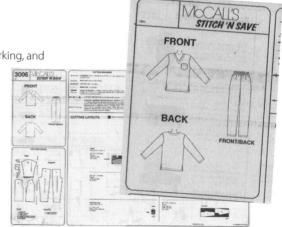

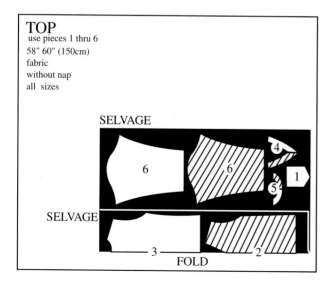

TOP
use pieces 1 thru 6
58" 60" (150cm)
fabric
without nap
all sizes

FABRIC KEY
RIGHT SIDE — WRONG SIDE — INTERFACING — LINING

SEWING DIRECTIONS
TOP

1. FRONT AND BACK

NOTE: Pocket is optional.

Finish upper edge of POCKET (1) with a zigzag stitch or turn under 1/4" (6mm) and edge-stitch with a conventional machine or overedge using an overlock machine (serger).

Symbols on a pattern are sewing and cutting "landmarks," similar to those found on a road map.

1 The **cutting line** is the solid, dark outer line. A scissors is sometimes printed on this line to let you know this is where you should cut.

2 The **stitching line** is the dotted line inside the cutting line. This is the line on which you stitch seams. (**Note:** This line may be omitted on multi-sized patterns.)

3 The **grainline arrow** is a straight line with an arrow at each end. It is used to position the pattern on the fabric. This arrow must be parallel to the fabric selvage or lengthwise grain. (For more detailed information, see pages 48-49.)

4 The **place on fold line** is narrower than the cutting line. This line tells you to position it on a fold of the fabric. The words "Place on fold" are usually printed along the line. Sometimes double-ended arrows point to the fold line.

5 The **notches** are single, double, or triple diamonds that help you match fabric pieces accurately as you sew.

6 The **circles and squares** are additional marks that help you match fabric pieces. Sometimes they show where to start or stop stitching.

7 The **hemline, center front** and **back**, and **fold line** show position and/or suggested sizes of special construction details.

> ## Nugget of Inspiration
> When shopping for your first pattern, keep it simple. Choose a pattern that doesn't have a lot of pattern pieces. If you're making a garment, look for one that isn't really fitted. An ideal first garment project is pajama pants. The pants are loose fitting, comfortable, and easy to sew. (See pages 127 to 130 for instructions on making pajama pants and coordinating tote bags.)

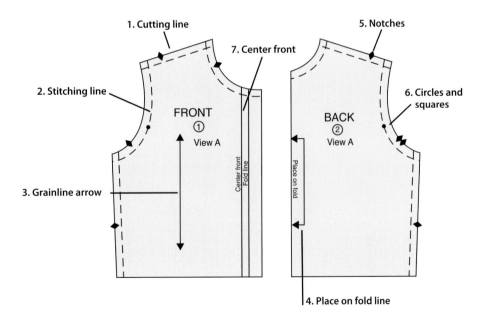

Labels: 1. Cutting line · 7. Center front · 5. Notches · 2. Stitching line · 6. Circles and squares · 3. Grainline arrow · 4. Place on fold line · FRONT ① View A · BACK ② View A · Center front Fold line · Place on fold

Measurements

Choosing a garment pattern depends on factors such as style preference, fabric choice, and even how much time you have to make the project. To know what size to buy, you need to determine your body measurements. Taking accurate measurements isn't difficult, but it is a crucial step in getting a good fit.

Follow these general guidelines when taking width measurements.
- Dress in a leotard or appropriate undergarments.
- Measure to the closest ½". Don't worry about differences of ¼" or less.
- Place a thumb or finger underneath the tape measure to prevent the measurement from being taken too tightly.
- Always keep the tape measure parallel to the floor.

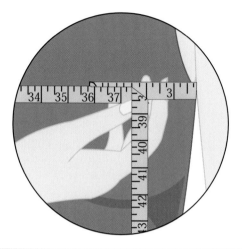

Take the following measurements:

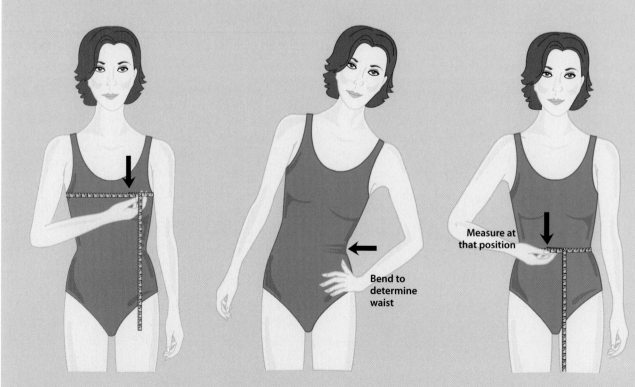

- **Bust:** Measure around the fullest part of the figure. Keep the tape measure parallel to floor.

- **Waist:** Bend to the side. The deepest wrinkle is your waist. Stand straight and measure around the waist at that position.

Motivating Memo Taking measurements by yourself can be challenging. Work with a fitting buddy. Invite a friend over and have her take your measurements. This is the best way to get accurate measurements.

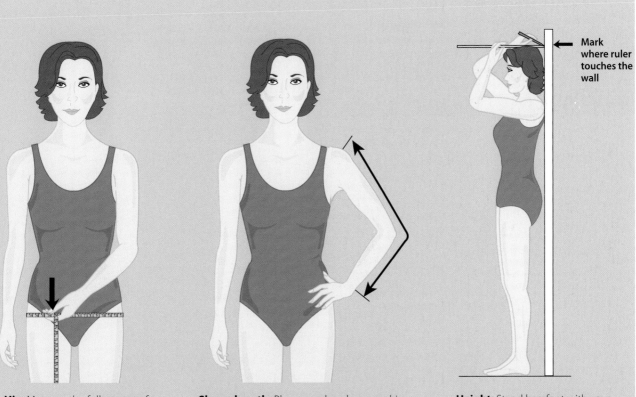

Mark where ruler touches the wall

• **Hip**: Measure the fullest part of the hip.

• **Sleeve length:** Place your hand on your hip. Feel for the knob at the end of your shoulder. Measure from that knob, over the elbow, to your wrist bone. This is important if your sleeve is usually too long or too short.

• **Height:** Stand barefoot with your back to a wall. Lay a ruler flat on top of your head. Mark where the ruler touches the wall, then measure from the mark to the floor.

Sizing and Alterations

For your first sewing projects, choose easy-fit garments such as pullover tops, easy-to-fit skirts, and pajama pants. The patterns will need very few – if any, changes. This section looks at the very basics of fitting – choosing the pattern size and a few time-honored pattern changes or alterations. For more detailed alterations and fitting ideas, visit sewingwithnancy.com.

Pattern Sizing

To determine your pattern size, compare your measurements to those in the size charts on the pattern. Choose the pattern size closest to your measurements. For tops, use the chest or bust measurement. If your measurements fall between sizes use the smaller size. It is always easier to increase the pattern at the bustline than to make a decrease.

For pull-on pants such as Pajama Pants, page 127, use the hip measurement. Since this is an easy-fit project, the only pants alteration addressed in this book is adjusting the length, making the pattern longer or shorter.

For easy-fit skirts, again use the hip measurement to determine the pattern size.

Nugget of Inspiration
The size pattern you need will generally be larger than your ready-to-wear size. Don't be alarmed and dive into a deep depression or a gallon of ice cream. This happens to everyone. The two sizing scales are just different, that's all.

Compare Measurements

Compare your measurements with those of your pattern. Create a simple fitting chart.

	Pattern measurement	Body measurement	Change needed + or -
Bust			
Waist			
Hip			
Pant length			
Sleeve length			

Nugget of Inspiration
If your comparison shows a ½" or less change, don't make an alteration. Measurements can change from one day to the next – especially after eating chocolate cake!

General Pattern Alteration Guidelines

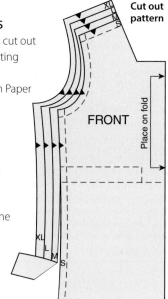

- If using a multi-sized pattern, cut out the pattern following the cutting lines for your size.
- Trace the pattern. Use Pattern Paper or a tissue paper worksheet. Make all alterations on that paper.
- Select two colors of fine point pens or pencils. On the following illustrations, a blue line indicates the original pattern outline, while a red line identifies the alterations.

Altering the Bust

If using a pattern size that's smaller than your bustline measurement, here's how to easily increase the pattern.

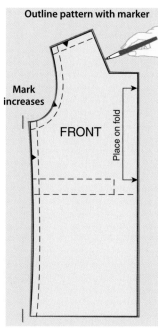

❶ Place the original pattern on top of the worksheet. Outline the pattern with the blue marker.

❷ Work with ½" increments. Divide the needed increase by four. (Two fabric edges, front and back, will be joined at each side seam—a total of four cut edges.) Divide the increase equally and add that amount to each of those four cut edges. For example, if you need a 2" increase, add ½" at each seam edge. (2" divided by 4 edges equals ½".)

❸ Measure and mark that distance from the outlined pattern at both the underarm cutting line and the hem edge.

❹ Place a pin at the shoulder where the armhole and shoulder seamlines cross. Pivot the pattern to meet the armhole increase mark. Trace the new armhole cutting line. This keeps the size of the armhole identical to that of the original pattern, so the sleeve fits perfectly.

❺ Move the pin to the underarm where the stitching lines cross. Pivot the pattern to meet the hip or lower edge increase. Trace the new cutting line between the underarm and the hemline.

❻ Match the pattern to the original outline and tape it to the worksheet.

❼ Repeat, making similar changes to the back pattern piece.

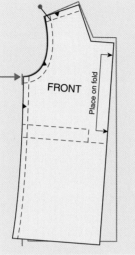

Pivot pattern to meet armhole increase

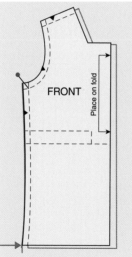

Pivot from underarm

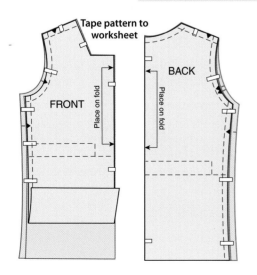

Tape pattern to worksheet

Altering the Waistline

When making a simple skirt pattern, purchase the pattern according to your hipline measurement. If your waistline needs an increase, here's an accurate, yet simple approach.

❶ Place the original pattern on top of the worksheet. Outline the pattern with a blue marker.

❷ Work with ½" increments. Divide the needed increase by four. Two fabric edges (front and back) will be joined at each side seam—a total of four cut edges. Divide the increase equally and add that amount to each of those four cut edges. Measure and mark that distance from the outlined pattern at the side seam waistline edge.

❸ Place a pin at the hipline (7" from the waistline for Junior and Half-sizes or 9" from the waistline for Misses sizes.) Pivot the pattern to meet the increase mark. Trace the new side seam between the hipline and waistline.

❹ Match the pattern to the original outline and tape to the worksheet. Repeat, making the same changes to the back pattern piece.

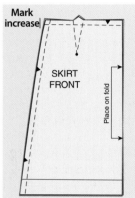

Mark increase

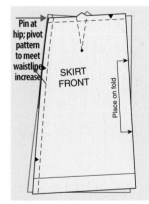

Pin at hip; pivot pattern to meet waistline increase

Nugget of Inspiration

If you increase the skirt waist measurement and your pattern includes a sew-on waistband, naturally you also need to increase the waistband. Add the total amount you added to the skirt itself—great fit, every time!

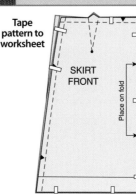

Tape pattern to worksheet

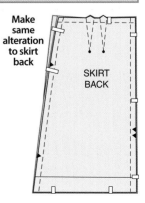

Make same alteration to skirt back

Lengthening or Shortening Pants

1️⃣ Place the original pants pattern front and back on a worksheet. Trace around only the lower edge and 1½" along each side seam with a marker.

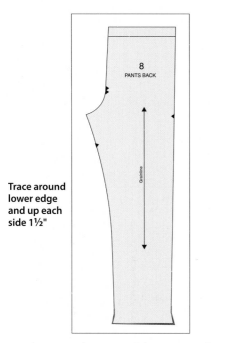

Trace around lower edge and up each side 1½"

2️⃣ Measure the required amount of change up or down from the hem.
- To lengthen the pants, measure up from the original hem.
- To shorten the pants, measure down from the original hem.

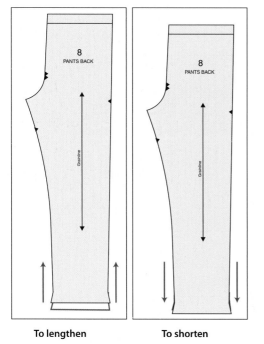

To lengthen   **To shorten**

3️⃣ Evenly slide the pattern up the required amount to lengthen the pants. Slide the pattern down to shorten the pants. Fold the excess pattern tissue out of the way.

4️⃣ Trace the remainder of the pants pattern.

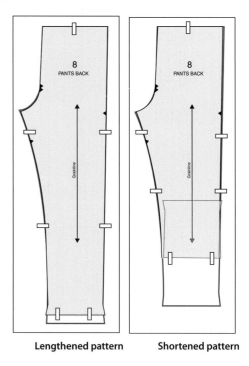

Lengthened pattern   **Shortened pattern**

Lengthening or Shortening Sleeves

Use the same steps detailed for changing the length of pants to alter sleeve lengths.

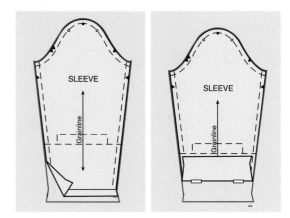

CHAPTER 5

Getting started is a matter of looking deep within and finding the desire to move forward. It means preparing for the journey ahead, choosing your path, and taking the first step toward your dreams. Then you take a deep breath and begin – with the realization that only you can accomplish your goals.

Getting Started

Layout

Accurately laying out the pattern is an essential part of constructing any project. The pattern guide sheet provides lots of valuable information. Take time to review it and lay out the pattern as it indicates.

Nugget of Inspiration

Follow the cutting layouts closely. Before actually cutting into your fabric, it's a good idea to test the layout, even if you don't have the table space to do it. The floor works just fine for this. That way you won't cut out half of the pattern and then realize that you laid it out incorrectly or didn't buy enough fabric.

1 Prepare the fabric.
- If your fabric is washable, double-check that you prewashed it before cutting. If not, see page 27 for instructions on prewashing fabric.
- Spread out your fabric. If it has a prominent center crease, press it out according to the care instructions. If this crease does not press out, adjust your cutting layout to avoid using the crease in your finished project.
- Carefully refold the fabric, matching the selvages and keeping the grainline straight.

2 Check the guide sheet to see which pieces you need for your selected view.

Motivating Memo The guide sheet is like a road map. It explains all the information you need from the start of a project to the finish. Refer to the guide sheet as you sew. It will answer many of your questions.

- Unfold the pattern pieces and take out those you need.
- If several pattern pieces are printed on the same sheet, cut out the pieces you need, leaving a margin of tissue around each piece. You'll trim the excess tissue to the cutting line when you cut out the project.
- Refold and put unneeded pattern pieces back in the pattern envelope.
- Press the pattern pieces with a warm dry iron to remove any wrinkles.

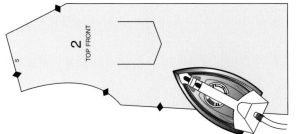

3 Select the correct layout on the pattern guide sheet.
- Find the view you are making.
- Find the fabric width.
- Find your size.

Motivating Memo Because it's easy to confuse all the different pattern layouts, circle the layout on the guide sheet for your size in the design view you've chosen. It's a simple step that eliminates frustration later.

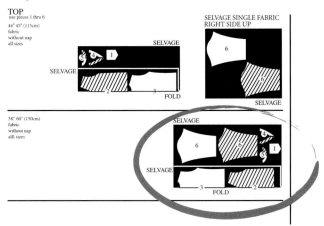

4 Fold the fabric as shown on the pattern layout.

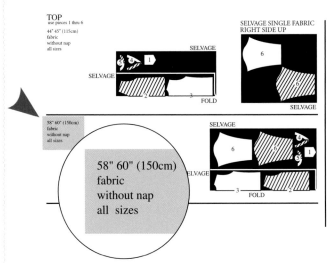

5 Lay the pattern pieces on the fabric.
- Place the larger pattern pieces first, following the guide sheet layout.
- Locate the grainline arrow. Pin one end of the arrow to the fabric. Measure the distance to the selvage.

- Measure the distance from the other end of the arrow to the selvage. Both distances must be the same. Pivot the pattern until the two distances are equal. Pin the second end of the arrow. The grainline is now parallel to the selvage.

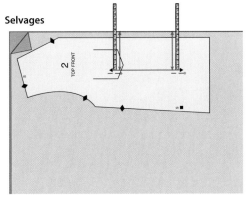

Selvages

Fold

Nugget of Inspiration

Don't mess around with the grainline. It might seem like a step that you can skip, especially if you're in a hurry or are worried about not having enough fabric. If you've ever tried on a piece of clothing that doesn't fit quite right, hangs awkwardly, or feels slightly twisted, you know what can happen when something is cut off grain. It really doesn't take that long to measure and position the pattern pieces correctly. If you think you're saving time or room by skipping that step, you're not. You're just jeopardizing your final results.

- If a pattern piece has a "place on fold" line, position that line exactly on the fold of the fabric. Pin the pattern to the fabric along the fold. Extend the pin tips beyond the fold so you don't accidentally cut along the fold of the fabric.

Selvages

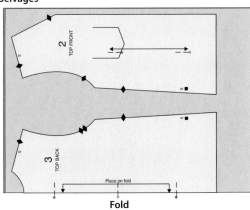

Fold

- Some pattern pieces may need to be placed on the fabric with their printed sides down. The guide sheet usually shows these pieces as shaded shapes.

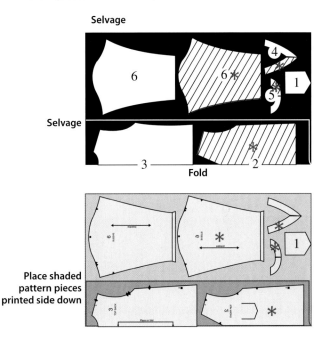

Selvage

Selvage

Fold

Place shaded pattern pieces printed side down

- The pattern pieces may be placed close together, but the cutting lines must not overlap.
- After placing all the pattern pieces on the fabric and straightening all the grainlines, smooth each piece and pin its corners. Place the pins diagonally.
- Add additional pins between the corners every 6" to 8". Use more pins around curved areas and on smaller pieces.
- Double check the guide sheet to make sure you've included all the pieces needed for the view you are making. Double check that the grainlines are straight.

Selvages

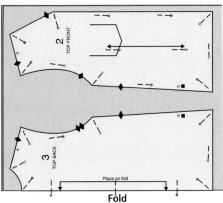

Fold

Cutting

When you're ready to cut out your fabric pieces, streamline your cutting sessions by following these timesaving strategies. They apply whether you cut with shears or a rotary cutter.

• Move around the fabric rather than moving the fabric toward you.

• Cut out each pattern piece, cutting along the marked pattern cutting line.

• Cut notches even with the cutting line. This gives a smoother line. Notches can be marked later.

• If the pattern calls for interfacing, cut out the interfacing at the same time you cut out the rest of the project. (See page 63 for more information about interfacing.)

• Cut out the pattern. Use a sharp scissors or shears, cutting with long, smooth strokes. For best results, use 8" dressmaker shears for cutting fabrics.

Nugget of Inspiration

To keep your sewing shears in good condition, don't *ever* use them to cut paper or anything else that isn't fabric. If you live with other people, train them to leave your sewing shears alone and always, always, always have a pair of paper cutting scissors around.

• Sharpen your sewing shears periodically to ensure clean-cut edges. Use a sharpening stone, sliding the stone upward along the beveled surface of the knife edge blade, working from the tip of the blade to the shank. After honing, wipe the blade clean (see page 6).

OR

• Cut out the pattern using a rotary cutter, cutting mat, and ruler.

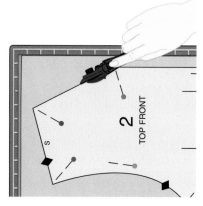

• Use a smaller cutter to cut out pattern pieces on light to medium weight fabrics; it provides greater maneuverability around curved areas than the larger size.

• Use a larger cutter for straight edges on heavier fabrics.

• A clear gridded ruler is helpful when cutting straight lines.

• Remember to close or retract the blade of the rotary cutter before putting it down. You don't want to accidentally cut yourself—or someone else.

If your pattern is the road map for your project, the notches, matching points, and other pattern details are the street signs. Once you've cut out all the pattern pieces, you must mark these details carefully and accurately in order to assemble your project efficiently. Use chalk, marking pens or pencils, or tracing paper and a tracing wheel to transfer markings from your pattern to the fabric.

❶ Transfer these markings:
  • Notches
  • Hemlines
  • Darts and pleats
  • Center front and center back
  • Dots, squares, button or pocket placements

❷ Markings are usually made on the fabric's wrong side. If you cut two layers at the same time, be sure to mark both layers.

Mark both sides

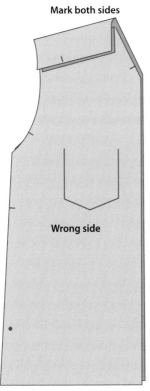

Wrong side

❸ An easy way to mark notches is with a washable marking pen or chalk pencil. Mark the notch with a short line perpendicular to the cut edge.

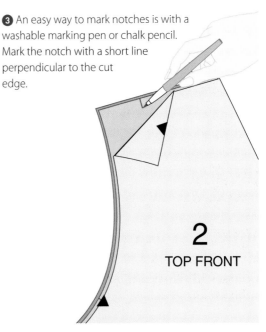

2
TOP FRONT

Motivating Memo As you gain more experience, try marking things like notches, outer edges of darts, center fronts and center backs, pleats, and hemlines with short nips. A nip is a ⅛" to ¼" long clip into the seam allowance, perpendicular to the seamline. The important part is the length of the clip. Don't cut too far! If you do, you will weaken the seam or have a hole in your project.

Motivating Memo Remember to test the marker on a scrap of fabric before using it on your project. You may want to try several types of markers before selecting one. Test to see what works best on your fabric.

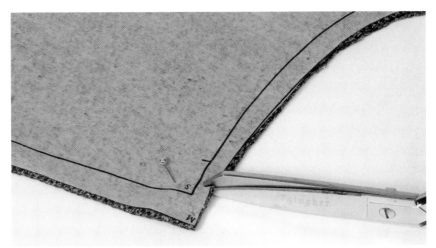

Cut short nips into the seam allowance.

4 To transfer markings with chalk or a marking pen:
- Poke a pin through each pattern dot or marking that needs to be transferred.

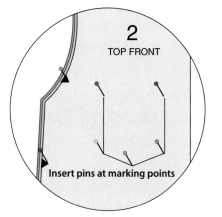

Insert pins at marking points

- Carefully remove the pattern from the fabric. Start at the outside pattern edges and work toward the center, pulling the pins gently through the pattern.
- Mark each pin's position. If you cut two layers of fabric at the same time, mark the wrong side of each layer.

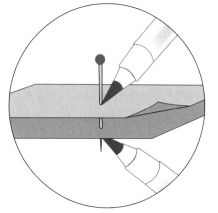

Mark each pin's position on each layer

Nugget of Inspiration

If you don't have a marking pen or marking chalk, resist the temptation to use a regular ink pen or crayon or marker or any other writing utensil you have lying around the house. It may solve the problem short term, but getting the ink out of the fabric may prove to be more difficult than you expected. Sometimes it might not come out at all. When marking fabric, it's better to be safe than sorry – buy a marking pen specifically designed to work on fabric.

5 To transfer markings with a tracing wheel and tracing paper:
- Use the lightest color sewing tracing paper that will show on your fabric. This is important, because tracing paper marks are sometimes difficult to remove.
- Place the colored side of the tracing paper next to the wrong sides of the fabric pieces.
- Always protect the table by placing cardboard under the fabric. The wheel's sharp points could damage some surfaces.

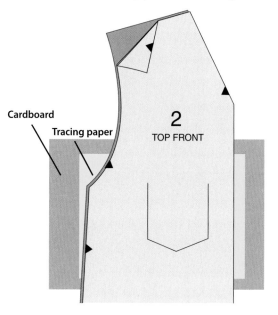

- Run the tracing wheel along the pattern markings. To more easily trace straight lines, place a ruler along the line and use it as a guide as you trace. Press firmly so the markings show on both layers. Test a fabric scrap before marking your project so you can tell how hard to press.

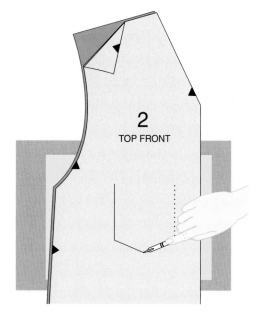

- After marking one area, reposition the tracing paper and cardboard. Continue until all the markings have been transferred.

6 If the right and wrong sides of your fabric look alike, mark the wrong sides before removing the pattern from the fabric. Mark an X on the wrong side with a marking pen or pencil or chalk. Or place a small piece of tape on the wrong side of the fabric.

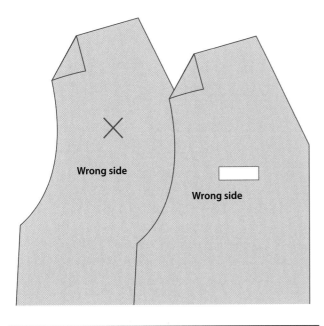

7 After transferring the markings, remove all the pattern pieces, press them with a dry iron, refold them, and put them neatly back into the pattern envelope.

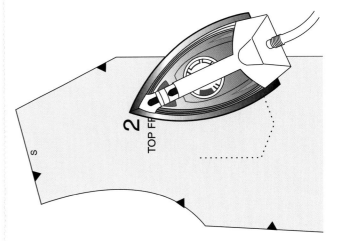

Nugget of Inspiration

Marking the wrong side may seem like an unnecessary step. That is, it will seem unnecessary until you finish a project only to realize that you sewed wrong sides together or sewed right to wrong sides. Making that little X on your fabric before you begin sewing could mean the difference between finishing the project in one evening or tearing the whole thing out and starting over. Which option sounds more fun to you?

Assembly

Your pattern guide sheet is your sewing road map. First read the instructions from start to finish to get an idea of the entire process. Check the fabric key on the guide sheet. Different shadings are used to show the right and wrong sides of the fabric and the interfacing. Then start at the beginning and complete each step.

• Place the guide sheet in an easy to see and reach location.

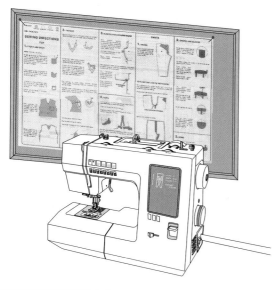

• After finishing a step, check it off on your guide sheet.

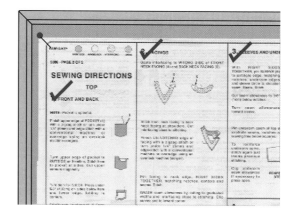

Motivating Memo I like to hang a bulletin board on the wall behind my sewing machine. I pin the guide sheet to the bulletin board so it will always be handy. Or pin the guide sheet to a curtain near your sewing area.

Nugget of Inspiration

If you plan to use your pattern multiple times, here are several options for keeping track of your progress and still having a clean copy the next time you use that pattern.

• Hang the guide sheet on a bulletin board. Use colored tacks or pins to mark each step as you complete it.

• Make a copy of the guide sheet. Check off each step as you do it.

• Use the original guide sheet, but use a pencil to mark each step. Erase the pencil marks when you're finished.

For most seaming, your stitches should be balanced. That means that the seam will look the same on the top and bottom layers. That should be true whether you're sewing a straight stitch or a zigzag stitch, or if you're serging an overlock seam.

On a sewing machine, the manufacturer usually presets the bobbin tension. Most machines have a tension regulator for controlling the tightness of the upper thread. Check your owner's manual for correct settings. Test stitching on a fabric scrap before working on your project. The needle and bobbin threads should interlock precisely at the center of the stitch, and the stitch should look the same on both the top and underside of the fabric. You may need to adjust the upper tension to get balanced stitches.

On a serger, manufacturers set the tensions for a balanced overlock stitch. The threads from the two loopers should interlock with the needle thread on the left and with each other at the fabric edge on the right. The needle thread(s) should hug the fabric and secure the looper threads without forming loops or causing puckers. Always test serging on a fabric scrap before serging on your project. You may need to adjust the looper tensions (and occasionally, the needle tension) to get balanced stitches.

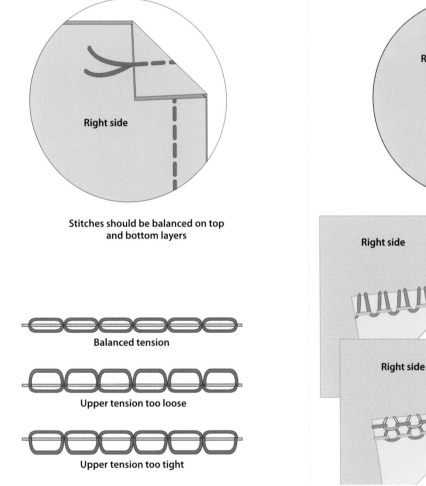

Stitches should be balanced on top and bottom layers

Balanced tension

Upper tension too loose

Upper tension too tight

Right side

Right side

Upper looper thread too tight

Lower looper thread too tight

If the upper tension is too tight, the needle thread will be taut on the fabric and the bobbin thread will be drawn to the top of the fabric. Loosen the upper tension to get a balanced stitch.

If the upper tension is too loose, the needle thread will be drawn to the underside of the fabric. Tighten the upper tension to get a balanced stitch.

If the upper looper is too tight, the lower looper thread will wrap to the top of the fabric. Reduce the upper looper tension to get a balanced stitch.

If the lower looper is too tight, the upper looper thread will wrap to the underside of the fabric. Reduce the lower looper tension to get a balanced stitch.

Seams

To complete most projects, you stitch a series of seams, which are formed by joining two fabric edges. The way you stitch seams on a conventional sewing machine varies, depending on whether your fabric is woven or knit.

Stitching Seams on Woven Fabrics

1 Set the stitch length at 2.5 to 3.0 (10 to12 stitches per inch).

2 Place the right sides of two pieces of fabric together, matching the seam edges, the top and bottom of the pieces, and the notches.

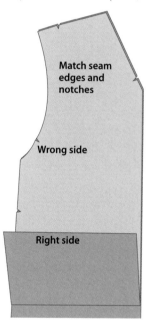

Match seam edges and notches

Wrong side

Right side

3 Pin the edges together.
- Place pins at right angles to the edge of the fabric.
- Pin heads should face the cut edge of the seam.
- Sew with the layer containing the pins on top.

4 Stitch the seam.
- Check the pattern's seam allowance. Most patterns allow ⅝" but some allow only ¼". It is important to stitch exactly on the seamline.

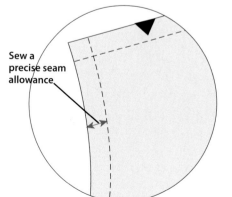

Sew a precise seam allowance

- Make sure the upper and bobbin threads are at the back of the machine, under the presser foot.

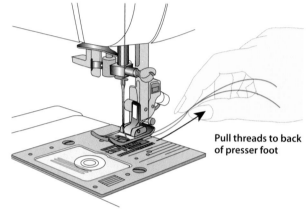

Pull threads to back of presser foot

- Place the end of the seam under the presser foot. Lower the presser foot.
- Lower the needle into the fabric by turning the balance wheel.
- Lock the stitches at the beginning and end of each seam to prevent them from coming out. To do this, sew two or three stitches then adjust the machine to stitch in reverse and sew two or three stitches. This is backstitching. Adjust the machine to stitch forward again and continue stitching. Guide the fabric so the seam is a uniform width.

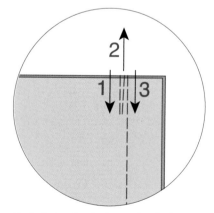

Backstitch at beginning and end of seam

- It's best to remove each pin as you come to it. Otherwise the machine needle could hit the pin, which could break or dull the needle.

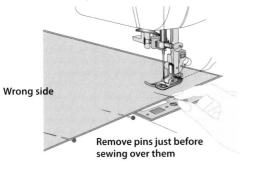

Wrong side

Remove pins just before sewing over them

- Stitch to the seam end and backstitch.

Motivating Memo Another way to lock stitching is to stitch in place several times. Set the stitch length lever at "0" and make two to three stitches. Then return the stitch length to 10 to 12 stitches per inch and continue stitching. Repeat the process at the end of the seam.

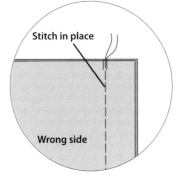

Stitch in place

Wrong side

- Turn the balance wheel until the take-up lever is at its highest point.

Raise take up lever to highest point

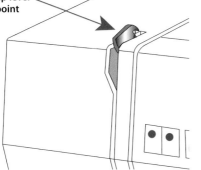

- Raise the presser bar lifter and pull the fabric to the back of the machine under the presser foot.
- Cut the threads close to the fabric. Leave 2" to 3" of thread coming from the machine needle.
- Trim the thread ends at the beginning of the seam close to the fabric.

Finishing Seams on Woven Fabric

Most woven fabrics ravel unless the edges are finished. After stitching a seam, add a seam finish to each seam edge to prevent fraying. Most seam finishes are done on a single thickness of fabric to avoid bulk and make the seam flatter and neater. Here are several ways to finish seams.

- Zigzag each seam edge.
  - Use a medium width zigzag and a medium-to-short stitch length.
  - Stitch the zig in the fabric and the zag close to or off the cut edge.
  - Zigzagging works best on medium to heavyweight fabrics. If zigzagging draws in the seam edge and makes it pucker, you may want to choose another seam finish.

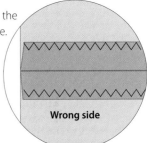

Wrong side

Motivating Memo If fabric edges always seem to curl and pucker when you zigzag, try using an overcast-guide foot. It has a center bar in the needle opening that keeps the fabric flat and prevents tunneling while the zigzag goes over the fabric edge.

Overcast-guide foot

- Serge each seam edge with a 3 thread or 3/4 thread serged overlock stitch.
- Edgestitch close to each seam edge. Set the machine to straight stitch. Guide the right edge of the presser foot along the cut edge of the fabric. (Stitching will be about ⅛" to ¼" from the cut edge.)

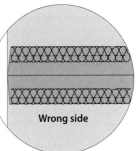

Wrong side

Motivating Memo

Edgestitching close to the seam edge is our least favorite option for seam finishing. However, this method may be your only choice if you don't own a serger and your machine has problems stitching a zigzag so close to the fabric edge.

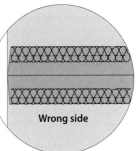

Wrong side

Stitching Seams on Knit Fabrics

❶ Pin the right sides of the two pieces of fabric together, matching the seam edges, tops and bottoms of the pieces, and notches.

❷ Straight stitch the seam or use a narrow zigzag. Use a straight stitch for vertical seams like side seams. Use a narrow zigzag (0.5 to 1.0 setting for width and length) for horizontal seams that go across or around your project. This allows the seam to stretch as the fabric does. Some knit patterns allow only ¼" seam allowances. Be sure to check the seam allowance recommended for your pattern.

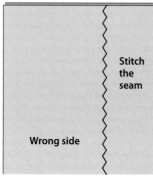

Stitch the seam

Wrong side

❸ Stitch the seam again, sewing ¼" away from the first stitching through both layers of fabric. A medium zigzag works best because it stretches like the fabric does.

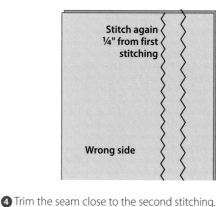

Stitch again ¼" from first stitching

Wrong side

❹ Trim the seam close to the second stitching.

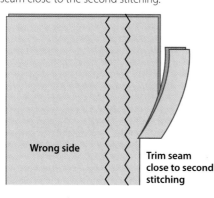

Wrong side

Trim seam close to second stitching

Serging an Overlock Seam

A serger can also be used to stitch a seam on knit or woven fabrics. A serged seam is stitched, trimmed, and finished in one step.

❶ First decide whether to use a serged seam or a conventional sewing machine seam with serged seam allowances.

- Use serged seams:
  - for most knit garments.
  - for loose-fitting garments where it isn't important for seams to lie flat.
  - when you're sure of the garment's fit and will not need to alter seams.
  - where seam allowances don't need to be pressed open.

Serged seam

¼"

Wrong side

- Use conventional seams with serged seam allowances:
  - with heavier, more bulky fabrics.
  - when you need wider seam allowances for inserting zippers or pockets.
  - when you're unsure of the fit and may need to alter seams.
  - when seams must be very flat and pressed open.

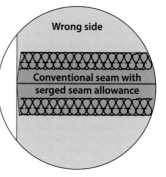

Wrong side

Conventional seam with serged seam allowance

❷ Pin the serged seams.

- Place pins the same direction as the seam rather than at right angles to the seam. If the pins are at right angles to the seam, the serger blade might hit the pin if it isn't removed and this could damage the blades as well as the pin.

- Place pins 1" from the seam edge so the serger foot will not pass over them.

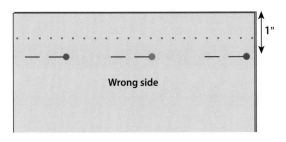

Wrong side

1"

❸ Serge the seams.
- A completed serged seam is only ¼" to ⅜" wide.
- If your pattern allows a ⅝" seam, you must determine where to position the fabric so the seam is sewn at the correct place.

Motivating Memo Some sergers have lines marked on the front of the machine to guide stitching. If your serger doesn't have these lines, place a mark or a strip of tape on the machine to show the stitching line.

- At the end of the seam, continue chain stitching for 2"–3", forming another thread tail. Then you're ready to serge another seam.

❹ Secure the seam ends.
- A serger does not backstitch, so you cannot secure seam ends by backstitching.
- Apply a dab of seam sealant such as FrayCheck or NoFray to the end of the seam to seal the threads. The liquid dries clear and prevents the thread ends from raveling. After it dries, cut off the thread tails.

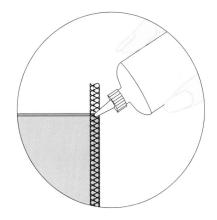

- Seams with corners are difficult to serge. Use a conventional sewing machine for these seams until you have more experience.

Pivoting

The technique used to turn corners is called pivoting.

1 Stitch to the corner. Stop with the needle down in the fabric. Lift the presser foot.

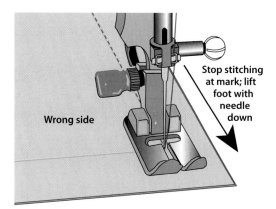

Wrong side

Stop stitching at mark; lift foot with needle down

2 Turn the fabric so the foot lines up with the next stitching line.

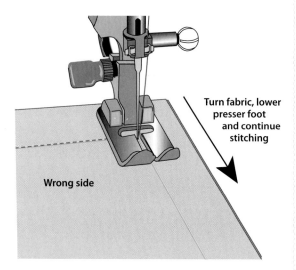

Turn fabric, lower presser foot and continue stitching

Wrong side

3 Lower the presser foot and continue stitching.

Motivating Memo When stitching heavy or bulky fabrics, you may get crisper, sharper corners if you take one or two stitches diagonally at the corner. Doing so provides room for the added bulk when you turn the corner right side out. I know—it sounds strange. But give it a try. You'll like the results.

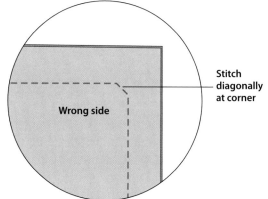

Wrong side

Stitch diagonally at corner

Nugget of Inspiration

Commercial patterns or instructions often tell you to pivot at corners. Wrapping the corner usually gives better results. See page 77 for details.

Pressing is just as important as sewing. Never delay pressing until the project is completed – always press every step of the way. Press each seam or construction detail before you cross it with another seam or construction detail.

- Pressing is different than ironing. In pressing, you lift the iron up and down. In ironing, you move the iron back and forth.
- When you press, use a steam iron or cover the fabric with a damp press cloth.
- Choose the correct iron temperature for your fabric.
- Press on the wrong side of the fabric.

Nugget of Inspiration

When pressing, always remember that irons generate a lot of heat. If you leave a hot iron in one place on your fabric too long, it will burn a hole in it or leave an ugly black burn mark. Either way, that's probably not something you planned for when designing the project. The moral of this story is always pay attention to what you're pressing.

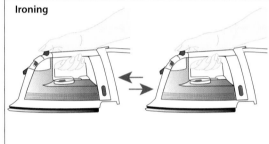

Pressing

Ironing

Pressing Seams Stitched with a Conventional Sewing Machine

- Press the seam flat. This sets the stitching and makes it easier to press the seam open.

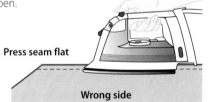

Press seam flat

Wrong side

- Place the seam over a seam roll and press it open. Using a seam roll prevents the seam edges from making an imprint on the right side of the fabric.

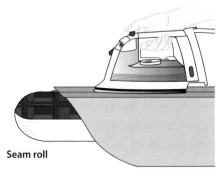

Seam roll

Pressing a Knit or Serged Seam

- Press the seam flat.

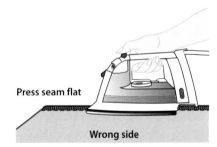

Press seam flat

Wrong side

- Position the seam over a seam roll and press to one side.
- To prevent seam imprints from showing on the right side of the fabric, place pieces of paper between the seam and the garment.

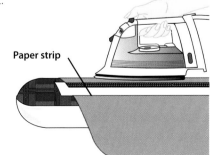

Paper strip

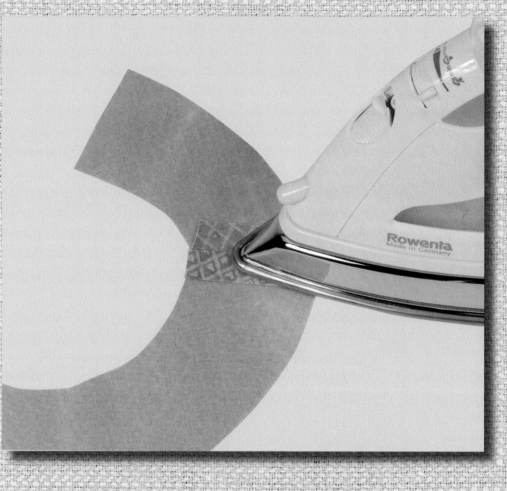

CHAPTER 6

Basic techniques are the building blocks of self-reliance, enabling you to achieve things you might never have thought possible. Knowledge of the basics empowers you to accomplish sewing tasks with boldness and conviction. Basic techniques give you the ability to create your own world, in whatever color, size, and pattern you choose.

Basic Techniques

Interfacing

Though not seen from the outside of your project, interfacing is a very important extra layer of fabric! It is fused to the wrong side of fabric to add shape and body.

Choose a fusible interfacing weight that's compatible with your fabric. Fusibles are available in weights ranging from very light for use with delicate lightweight fabrics, to heavy for use with woolens and wool blends. Check the instructions included with the interfacing or the label on the end of the bolt for use suggestions.

Choose fusible interfacing one weight lighter than your fabric since the fusing resins add weight when the interfacing is fused to the fabric. For example, if using a medium weight fabric, choose a lightweight fusible interfacing.

Fusible Interfacing Test Swatch

To determine whether a fusible is suitable for your fabric and how long it will take to fuse, make a test swatch.

❶ Cut a 4" square of both the fusible interfacing and fabric.

❷ Place the rougher side of the interfacing next to the wrong side of the fabric.

❸ Position a 1" square of fabric at one corner, between the fabric and interfacing. Use this fabric square as a "handle" to test the fused fabrics.

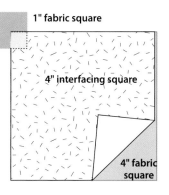

1" fabric square

4" interfacing square

4" fabric square

❹ Follow the manufacturer's instructions to apply the interfacing. In general, cover with a damp cloth and fuse the interfacing for 10 to 15 seconds, using a steam iron set at the wool temperature.

❺ After the test square cools, try to peel the interfacing from the fabric using the 1" fabric handle. If you can easily separate the layers, the interfacing did not fuse properly. Increase fusing time, pressure, and/or temperature.

❻ Check the appearance of the interfaced test square. Look for bubbles, wrinkles, or discoloration on the right side of the fabric square. Also check the drape and feel of the interfaced fabric. Has the interfacing added too much weight? If so, test a lighter weight interfacing.

Fuse Interfacing to the Fabric

❶ Interface the entire fabric piece. This is called a full fuse. Cut interfacing to the pattern size.

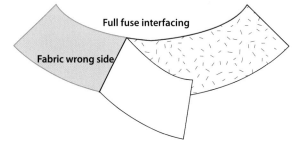

Full fuse interfacing

Fabric wrong side

❷ Center the interfacing on the fabric, placing the rough side of the interfacing next to the wrong side of the fabric.

❸ Cover the interfacing with a damp press cloth.

❹ Use the tip of the iron to steam baste the interfacing, securing it to the fabric in a few key areas.

❺ Fuse the interfacing following the manufacturer's instructions.

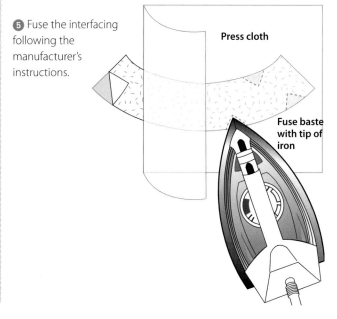

Press cloth

Fuse baste with tip of iron

Adding Facings

A facing covers and encloses a raw edge. It usually doesn't show on the outside of the garment. You may find facings at the neckline, armhole, sleeve, front, and back openings.

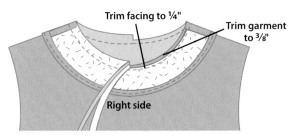

1 Fuse interfacing to the wrong side of the facing sections.

2 If the facing has several sections, follow the pattern directions for stitching them together. Press the seams open and trim them to ¼" to reduce bulk.

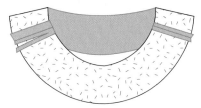

3 Finish the outer edge of the facing by zigzagging, serging, or clean finishing the edges.

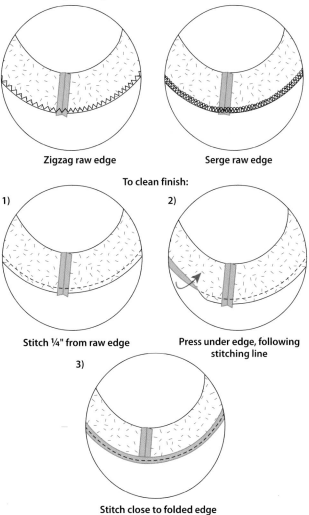

Zigzag raw edge   **Serge raw edge**

To clean finish:

1)

2)

Stitch ¼" from raw edge   **Press under edge, following stitching line**

3)

Stitch close to folded edge

4 Stitch the facing to the garment, right sides together, aligning the cut edges and matching the notches, seams, and markings.

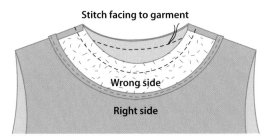

Stitch facing to garment

Wrong side

Right side

5 Cut each seam allowance a different width to reduce bulk all the way around the neckline. This is called grading.
- Trim the facing seam to ¼".
- Trim the garment seam to ³⁄₈".

Trim facing to ¼"

Trim garment to ³⁄₈"

Right side

Motivating Memo Use pinking shears to grade and trim the seam allowances in one step. When using lightweight fabrics, trim both seam allowances simultaneously. To minimize bulk when using heavier fabrics, cut each seam allowance separately.

- If the seam has a sharp or pronounced curve, you may need to clip the seam to make it lie flat after the facing is turned to the wrong side. Cut short nips perpendicular to the seamline. Be careful not to clip past the seamline.

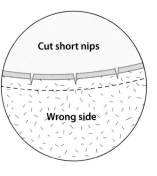

Cut short nips

Wrong side

Motivating Memo Less is best! Try to avoid clipping when possible, as it weakens a seam and creates an indented curve. Yet it is necessary on small areas such as children's or doll clothes.

6 Understitch as follows, stitching both seam allowances to the facing. Understitching prevents the facing from rolling to the right side.

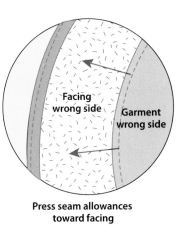

Facing wrong side

Garment wrong side

Press seam allowances toward facing

- Press the seam flat, then press the facing away from the garment, covering the seam allowance. Press all the seam allowances toward the facing.
- From the right side, stitch the seam allowances to the facing with either a straight stitch, zigzag, or multi-step zigzag. Stitch on the facing, close to the seamline.

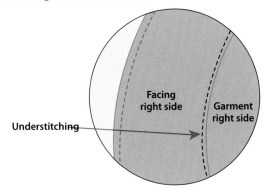

Understitching

Facing right side

Garment right side

Motivating Memo Try using a multi-step zigzag for understitching. Instead of just zigzagging back and forth, the machine makes several stitches for each zig and zag. This helps the facing lie smooth. Check your instruction manual to see if your machine can sew this stitch.

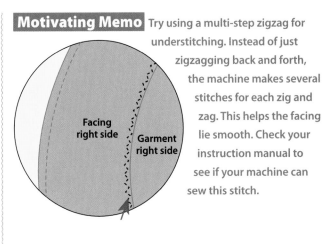

Facing right side

Garment right side

7 Turn the facing to the wrong side and press.

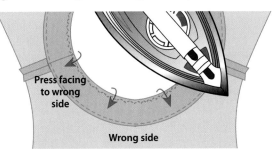

Press facing to wrong side

Wrong side

8 Secure the facing to the garment at the seamlines. Stitch in the ditch as follows to prevent the facing from rolling to the right side.
- Stitch in the groove (called the ditch) of each seam. Stitch from the right side, sewing through all the thicknesses.

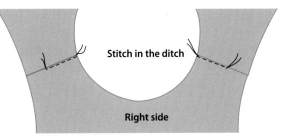

Stitch in the ditch

Right side

- Stitch the full width of the facing. Pull the thread tails to the wrong side and tie. Clip off the thread tails.

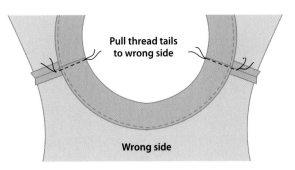

Pull thread tails to wrong side

Wrong side

Casings

Making a casing is a simple technique that you'll find in many projects along your sewing journey. Whether you're making a pair of elastic-waist pants, a set of curtains for your home, or a drawstring bag, mastering this technique will help you complete the project in no time flat.

❶ Finish the outer edge of the fabric by zigzagging, serging, or clean finishing the edge. (See page 64 for more details.)

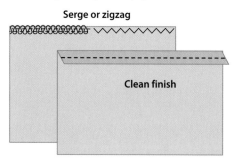

Serge or zigzag

Clean finish

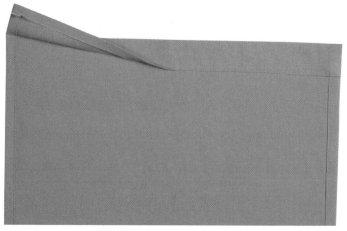

❷ Fold and press the casing the desired width. (If this measurement is not marked on your pattern, make sure it's wider than whatever you will insert into the casing, such as a curtain rod or elastic.)

❸ Pin the casing. Place pins at right angles to the stitching line, with the heads facing the fold.

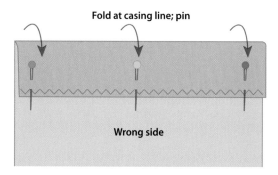

Fold at casing line; pin

Wrong side

Motivating Memo To see this technique in action, turn to the project section at the back of the book. Try your hand at the curtains on page 109, the pajama pants on page 127, or the drawstring bag on page 130.

Nugget of Inspiration

To give curtains a dash of pizzazz, use one of your machine's decorative stitches for stitching the casing. You might also try using a contrasting color of thread. This is a simple way to add a unique touch to your curtains and spice up what is normally strictly functional (and not very exciting).

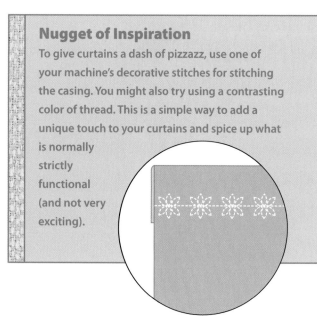

❹ Stitch along the upper and lower edges of the casing.

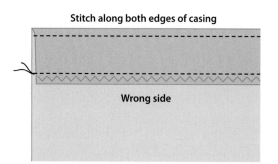

Stitch along both edges of casing

Wrong side

Elastic Waistband

For wearing comfort, there's nothing like an elastic waistline. Elastic adjusts easily whether you're performing yoga poses or running errands. The following tips will make an easy task even easier.

1 Finish the top edge by zigzagging, serging, or clean finishing the edge. (See page 64 for more details.)

2 Press under the casing width (generally 1½") along the top edge of the pants or skirt before stitching the side seams.

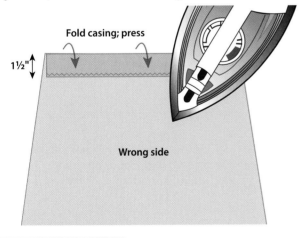

Fold casing; press

1½"

Wrong side

Motivating Memo Doing this pressing while the fabric is still flat is definitely easier than working in a circle later. This initial pressing provides a guide for the casing line; it may be all that's needed when you finish the casing later.

3 Stitch the side seams, as well as any center front and back seams.
- Open up the pressed casing so the fabric is again flat.
- On **one** of the seams, stop stitching and backstitch at the casing line. Advance the thread and add a few stitches close to the cut edge, leaving approximately 1¼" unstitched to provide an opening for inserting the elastic.
- Press the seams flat, then open.

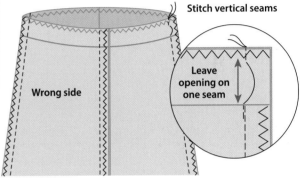

Stitch vertical seams

Wrong side

Leave opening on one seam

4 Machine baste the seam allowances to the garment to prevent the elastic from getting caught during insertion. Start at the upper edge and stitch about 3".

Baste seam allowances to garment

Wrong side

5 Stitch the casing.
- Refold the casing to the wrong side. Stitch close to the folded edge.
- Add a second row of stitching near the cut edge of the casing.

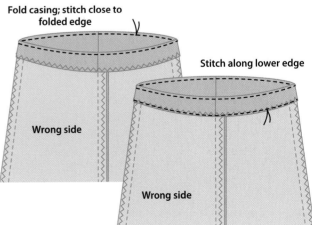

Fold casing; stitch close to folded edge

Stitch along lower edge

Wrong side

Wrong side

6 Insert the elastic.

- Cut 1" or 1¼" wide elastic approximately 2" smaller than your waistline measurement. Put the elastic around your waistline to make sure it's comfortable. Adjust the length if needed.
- Zigzag one end of the elastic to a sturdy woven fabric scrap that is wider than the elastic to help prevent the elastic from being drawn into the casing.

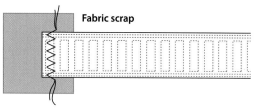

Fabric scrap

- Attach an E/Z Feeder Guide or safety pin to the unstitched end of the elastic. Thread the elastic through the opening, being careful not to twist or turn the elastic.

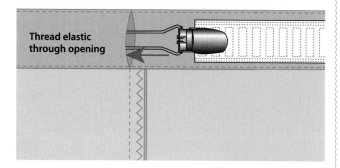

Thread elastic through opening

- After the elastic is threaded through the casing, butt the unstitched end against the first end of the elastic. Zigzag through the elastic and fabric several times.
- Trim away the extra fabric that extends beyond the elastic. The joining will be flat and not bulky.
- Distribute the fullness evenly. Stitch in the ditch at each side seam to keep the elastic evenly distributed and prevent the elastic from twisting or rolling.
- Remove the basting stitches.

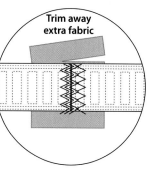

Trim away extra fabric

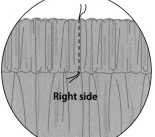

Distribute fullness; stitch in the ditch at side seams

Right side

Face the Waistline

This waistband technique is ideal for simple skirts or pants with smooth, bulk-free, and contemporary styling. The process is very similar to adding a facing to a top.

1 Apply fusible interfacing to the wrong side of the facing.

2 Stitch the facing side seams.

- Meet the back facings to the front facing with right sides together, matching the notches. Stitch the side seams.

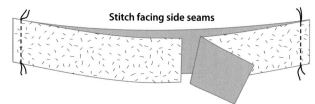

Stitch facing side seams

- Press the seams flat, then open.
- Trim the seams to ¼" to reduce bulk.

3 Finish the lower edge of the facing by zigzagging, serging, or clean finishing the edge. (See page 64 for more details.)

4 Meet the facing to the garment with right sides together, meeting the cut edges, notches, and seams. Turn under the back edges of the facing at the zipper; stitch.

Turn under facing edges; stitch

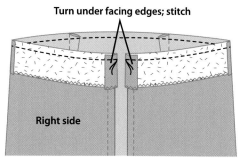

Right side

5 Grade the seam allowances, trimming the facing seam to ¼" and the garment seam to ⅜". (See page 64 for more details.)

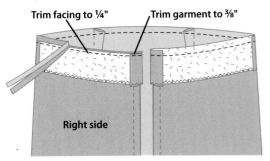

Trim facing to ¼" Trim garment to ⅜"

Right side

6 Understitch, stitching both seam allowances to the facing to prevent the facing from rolling to the right side.

• Press the seam flat, then press the facing away from the garment, covering the seam allowance. Press all seam allowances toward the facing.

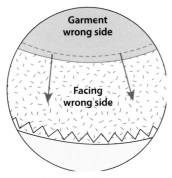

Garment wrong side

Facing wrong side

Press facing away from garment

• From the right side, stitch the seam allowances to the facing with either a straight stitch, zigzag, or multi-step zigzag. Stitch on the facing close to the seamline.

Understitching

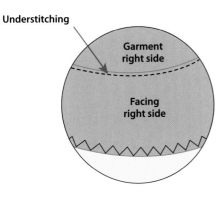

Garment right side

Facing right side

Motivating Memo Try using a multi-step zigzag for understitching. Instead of just zigzagging back and forth, the machine makes several stitches for each zig and zag. This helps the facing lie smooth. Check your instruction manual to see if your machine can sew this stitch.·

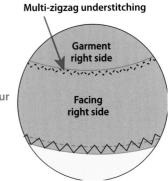

Multi-zigzag understitching

Garment right side

Facing right side

7 Turn the facing to the wrong side and press.

8 Hand stitch the center back facing edges to the zipper tapes. *Optional:* Topstitch close to the upper edge of the garment.

Topstitch upper edge

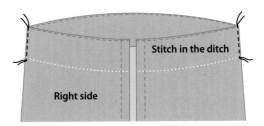

Wrong side

9 Secure the facing to the garment at the side seamlines. Stitch in the ditch to prevent the facing from rolling to the right side.

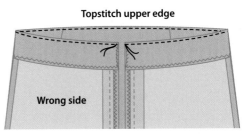

Stitch in the ditch

Right side

• Stitch in the groove (ditch) of each seam. Stitch from the right side, sewing through all the thicknesses.

• Stitch the full width of the facing. Pull the thread tails to the wrong side and knot. Clip off the thread tails.

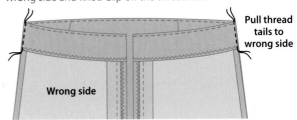

Pull thread tails to wrong side

Wrong side

Sew-on Waistband

A separate waistband on a skirt or pants looks great, but it can add bulk. And who needs more bulk at the waistline? This waistband technique eliminates bulk by removing part of the seam allowance before you cut the band.

1 Insert a zipper in the side or center seam. (See page 87 for details.)

2 Modify and cut out the waistband.
- Fold under ½" along the long unnotched edge of the waistband pattern.

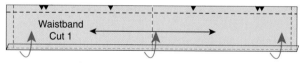

Fold under ½" along unnotched edge

- Align the folded edge of the waistband pattern along the ravel-free fabric selvage if possible. If you can't place the band on the selvage, finish the edge by zigzagging or serging.
- Cut out the waistband, marking the notches and centers.

3 Interface the waistband.
- Fuse interfacing to the wrong side of the waistband.
- Fold and press the waistband along the fold line with wrong sides together.

4 Stitch the waistband to the garment with right sides together, matching the notches and centers. The waistband will extend beyond the garment on each end.
- Grade the seam allowances, trimming the waistband seam to ¼" and the garment seam to ⅜". (See page 64 for more details.)
- Angle cut the skirt seam allowances and darts from the stitching line to the cut edge to reduce bulk.

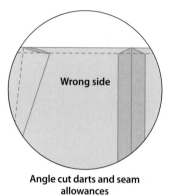

Angle cut darts and seam allowances

- Cut off any excess zipper tape. Securely zigzag over the ends of the zipper tape to reinforce them.
- Press the seam flat, then press the waistband up, covering the seam.

Cut off excess zipper tape

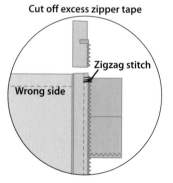

5 Fold the waistband along the fold line with right sides together (the lower edges won't meet). The selvage/finished edge extends ⅛" below the stitched seamline.

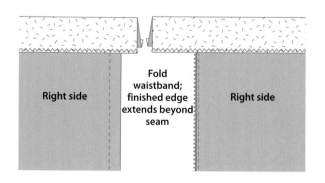

6 Finish the waistband ends.

- Stitch the end seams. On the left end, stitch straight up from the zipper overlap. The right end extends beyond the zipper. Stitch, using a conventional seam allowance.

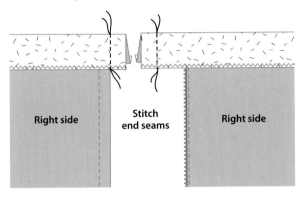

- Trim and grade the seam allowances. Angle cut the corners.
- Turn the waistband right side out. The selvage/finished edge of the band will extend slightly below the waist seam.

Turn band right side out

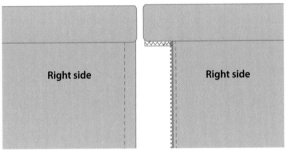

7 Turn the waistband right side out. Use a Bamboo Pointer and Creaser to help get sharp corners. Press the band so the fold line is at the top of the band.

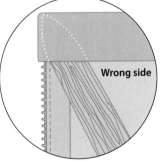

Bamboo Pointer and Creaser

8 Finish the band.

- Pin the remaining edge of the band over the waist seam. The selvage/finished edge of the band will extend slightly below the waist seam. Pin from the right side of the garment.

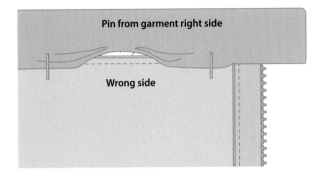

- Topstitch the waistband, or stitch in the ditch, stitching from the right side. To stitch in the ditch, straight stitch in the groove (called the ditch) of the seam. The stitching will blend into the seam and will not be noticeable from the right side. On the wrong side the stitching will catch the remaining waistband edge.

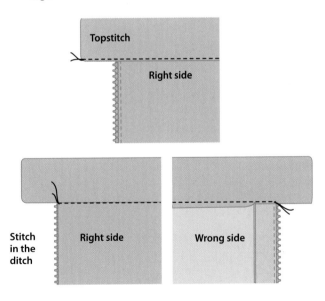

Gathering

Gathering is used to ease in extra fabric on a larger piece of fabric so it can be joined to a smaller piece of fabric. Gathering is often used in home dec projects, or on garments at places like a waistline or a yoke. Here are two easy ways to gather.

Gathering Over a Cord

This technique is especially helpful when the fabric that will be gathered is very long or if the fabric is heavy or stiff.

❶ Cut a piece of strong string or cord 3" to 6" longer than the fabric that will be gathered.

❷ Place the cord on the wrong side of the fabric, ½" from the cut edge. Several inches of cord should extend at each end.

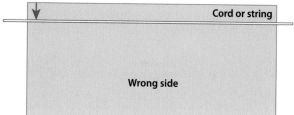

Place cord ½" from edge

Cord or string

Wrong side

❸ Set the sewing machine for a wide zigzag stitch.

❹ Zigzag over the cord from end to end. *Do not* stitch through the cord.

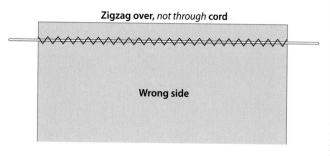

Zigzag over, *not through* **cord**

Wrong side

❺ Fasten one end of the cord by wrapping it around a pin in a figure 8.

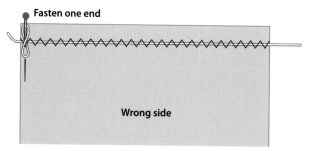

Fasten one end

Wrong side

❻ Pull the other end of the cord, gathering the fabric until it is the same size as the edge to which it will be joined. Fasten the cord end by wrapping it around a pin in a figure 8.

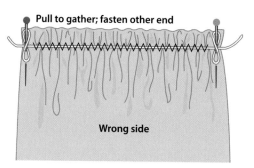

Pull to gather; fasten other end

Wrong side

❼ Slide and adjust the gathers until they are evenly spaced.

❽ Pin the right side of the gathered section to the right side of the ungathered section, meeting the cut edges and notches.

❾ Stitch the seam with the gathered side facing up. This makes it easier to control the gathers and get them even.

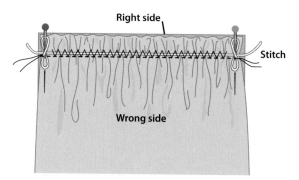

Right side

Stitch

Wrong side

Using Two Rows of Machine Stitching

This gathering technique is especially helpful for very lightweight fabrics.

1 Change the machine stitch length to basting, about six stitches per inch.

2 Stitch one row of basting ⅝" from the cut edge. Leave the thread tails 2" to 3" long at the beginning and end of the stitching.

3 Stitch a second basting row ¼" from the cut edge.

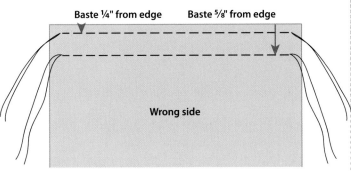

Baste ¼" from edge   Baste ⅝" from edge

Wrong side

Leave 2"–3" thread tails

4 Fasten the bobbin threads at one end of the stitching by wrapping them around a pin in a figure 8.

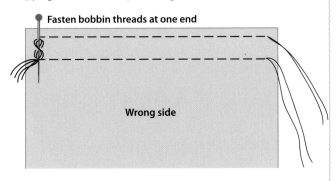

Fasten bobbin threads at one end

Wrong side

5 At the other end of the stitching, pull both bobbin threads. Gather the fabric until it is the same size as the edge to which it will be stitched.

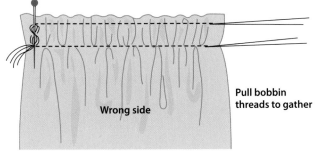

Wrong side

Pull bobbin threads to gather

6 Fasten the threads by wrapping them around a pin in a figure 8.

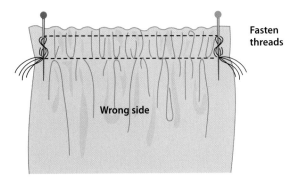

Fasten threads

Wrong side

7 Slide and adjust the gathers until they are evenly spaced.

8 Pin the right side of the gathered section to the right side of the ungathered section, meeting the cut edges and notches.

9 Stitch the seam with the gathered side facing up. This makes it easier to control the gathers and get them even.

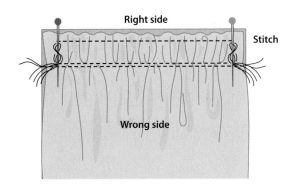

Right side

Stitch

Wrong side

Darts

Darts are triangular folds of fabric with wide ends that taper to a point. They help shape a garment so it fits around curves such as body contours. You can quickly sew a smooth and durable dart using the following steps.

1 Mark the dart.

• Using a fabric marking pen or chalk on the fabric wrong side, mark the outer ends and the point of each dart. (Or mark the ends with nips and the point with a pin.)

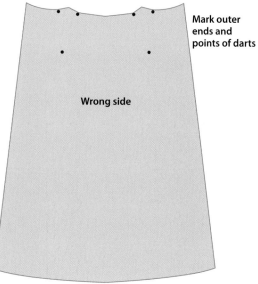

Mark outer ends and points of darts

Wrong side

• Fold the dart with right sides together, matching the dart's outer ends.

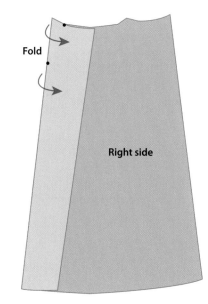

Fold

Right side

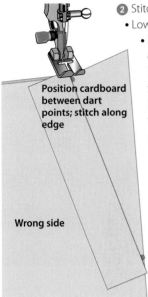

Position cardboard between dart points; stitch along edge

Wrong side

② Stitch the dart.
- Lower the needle into the fabric.
  - Find a piece of lightweight cardboard or paper at least as long as the dart. Before lowering the presser foot, place the paper between the ends and the point of the dart.
  - Starting at the wide end of the dart, backstitch or stitch in place several times to lock the stitching.
  - Lengthen the stitch to normal length and using the cardboard as a guide, finish stitching the dart.
  - At the end of the dart, turn the machine's wheel by hand, sewing three to four stitches along the fold.
- Stitch off the fabric 1" to 2", forming a chain of thread. Secure the chained thread tail by sewing two or three stitches in place in the dart. Trim the thread ends.

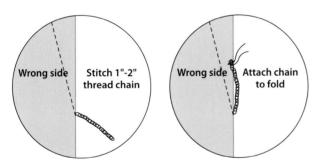

Wrong side — **Stitch 1"-2" thread chain**

Wrong side — **Attach chain to fold**

③ Press the dart flat, stopping ½" from its point.
- Open the fabric and press the dart over a ham. The ham is rounded and curved like your body, so it helps shape the dart.

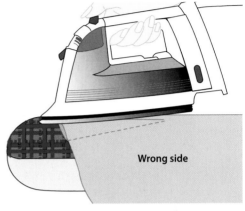

Wrong side

- Press vertical darts toward the center front or center back.
- Press horizontal darts downward.

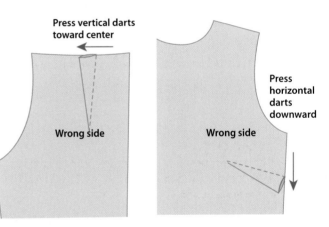

Press vertical darts toward center

Wrong side

Press horizontal darts downward

Wrong side

Nugget of Inspiration

Most people's bodies are not perfectly straight; they have curves. As you gain more confidence using this technique and feel more comfortable stitching darts, go ahead and bend the rules a bit. Try stitching the dart with a slight curve instead of a straight line so the garment conforms to your body shape better. Stitching closer to the fold results in a convex (outward) curve; stitching away from the fold results in a concave (inward) curve. You may want to stitch a few practice darts first and hold them up to your body until you get the curve just right. The time will be well spent – you'll end up with more flattering clothing that really fits.

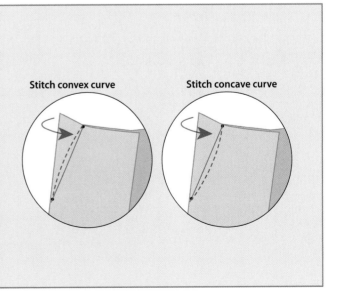

Stitch convex curve

Stitch concave curve

Pleats

Think of a pleat as a mini-dart with no point at the end. It's easy to stitch pleats using the same techniques as for darts.

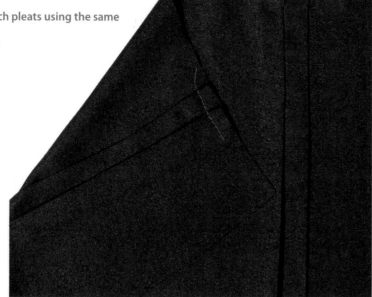

① Mark pleats using short ⅛" nips at the ends and fabric marking pen dots at the tips.

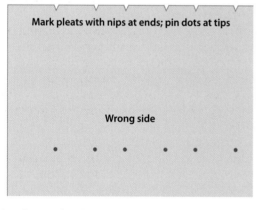

Mark pleats with nips at ends; pin dots at tips

Wrong side

② Pin the pleats with right sides together, matching the nips and dots.

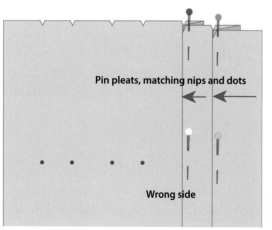

Pin pleats, matching nips and dots

Wrong side

③ Some pleats are stitched for several inches, while others may only be secured in a seam at the upper edge. For stitched pleats, position the edge of a piece of cardboard between the nips and dots. Lock the stitches at the top of the pleat and stitch along the cardboard edge.

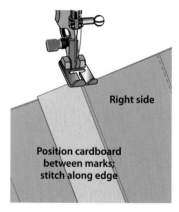

Right side

Position cardboard between marks; stitch along edge

④ Press the pleat underlays toward the side seams. This is the opposite of pressing darts, but gives a more attractive appearance.

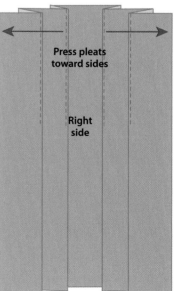

Press pleats toward sides

Right side

Many sewing projects include corners. You'll find corners on collars and cuffs, and on home dec projects such as throw pillows, pillowcases, and gift bags. You'll be pleased with the crisp corners you can achieve using this wrapped corner technique.

1 Meet two fabric sections with right sides together.

2 Stitch one edge.

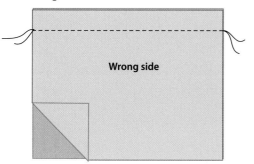

3 Press the seam allowance flat, then fold the seam toward the center along the stitching line and press again. This wraps the seam allowance and makes it easier to produce sharp corners and crisp edges.

4 Stitch, starting from the folded edge, creating a wrapped corner.

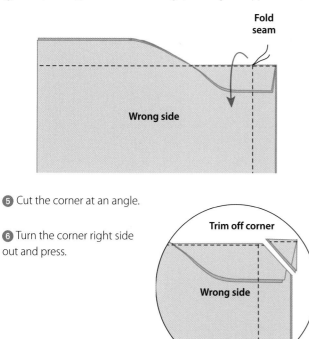

5 Cut the corner at an angle.

6 Turn the corner right side out and press.

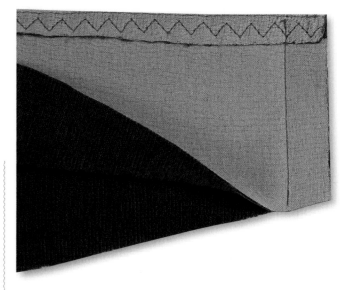

Wrapped Corner Collar

Here's how to get a picture-perfect collar using the wrapped corner technique.

Some patterns tell you to cut one collar section, while others have you cut two. Use this wrapped corner technique for both.

Most guide sheet instructions call for interfacing on only one collar layer – the under collar when you cut two, and the half of the collar closest to the neckline when you use one. But interfacing both the upper and under collar adds body and makes the collar seam stronger.

1 Cut out fusible interfacing for the entire collar, whether one piece or two. Fuse the interfacing to the wrong sides of the collar.

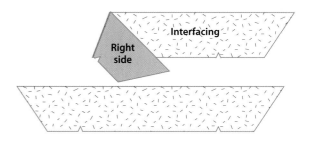

Motivating Memo With a two-piece collar, your pattern instructions may tell you to pivot at the corners of the collar and to stitch the entire seam with one stitching. It's much easier to stitch the ends and the outer edge in separate steps. Try it! You'll have success every time.

2 With a two-piece collar, pin the collar pieces together along the unnotched edge with right sides together. Stitch the seam from end to end.

Stitch along unnotched edge

3 Press the seam flat, then open. This helps give the collar a crisp finished edge.

4 Grade the under collar seam allowance to ¼" and the upper collar seam allowance to ⅜".

Trim under collar to ⅛" **Trim upper collar to ⅜"**

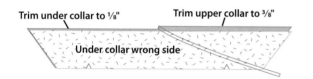

5 Press the seam allowances toward the under collar and understitch the entire seam. (For more details, see page 65.)

Motivating Memo When sewing medium weight or heavier fabric, use a multi-zigzag stitch for the understitching. It gives more stitches per inch than a regular zigzag, creating a crisper collar edge. If your sewing machine doesn't have a multi-zigzag stitch, use a regular zigzag.

Multi-zigzag understitching **Upper collar right side** **Under collar right side**

6 Fold the collar along the seamline with right sides together. The seam allowances will wrap toward the under collar.

7 Stitch from the fold to the neckline edge. Repeat, stitching the other end of the collar in the same way.

Fold along seamline; stitch ends

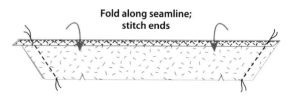

8 To reduce bulk, grade the seam allowances and trim the corners at an angle. Press the seams to one side and then press them open.

Grade seam allowances and trim corners

9 Turn the collar right side out. Use a Bamboo Pointer and Creaser to help form sharp corners. Press the collar.

Right side

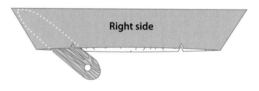

For a one-piece collar, interface the entire collar. Fold the collar along the fold line with right sides together and follow Steps 7 to 9 above.

There are two general types of sleeves: a shirt sleeve and a cap sleeve.

• A shirt sleeve has less slope, a shorter cap, and less ease than a traditional cap sleeve.

• A cap sleeve has a greater slope, higher cap, and more ease than a shirt sleeve. It must always be eased to fit the armhole.

A sleeve generally has one notch indicating the front of the sleeve and two notches indicating the back. A circle marking indicates the position for the shoulder seam. Be sure to transfer these three markings to the sleeve and the garment.

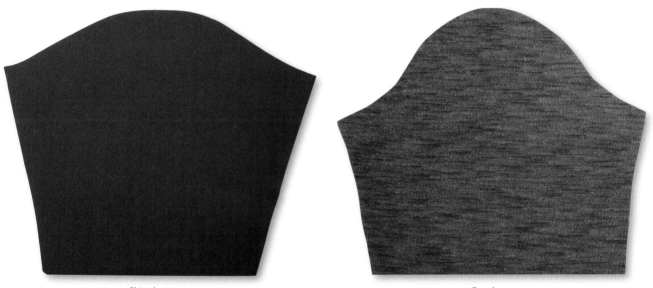

Shirt sleeve.　　　　　　　　　　　　　　　*Cap sleeve.*

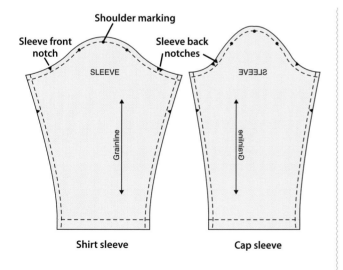

Shirt sleeve　　　　Cap sleeve

Motivating Memo If the right and wrong sides of your fabric look alike, mark an X on the wrong side with a marking pen or pencil or chalk. Or place a small piece of tape on the wrong side of the fabric to prevent two "left" sleeves.

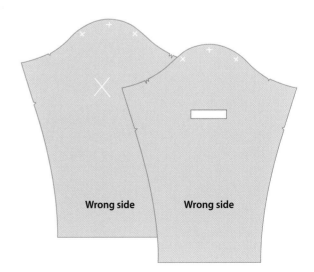

Wrong side　　　　Wrong side

Shirt Sleeve Construction

Inserting a shirt sleeve is easy using this flat construction technique. The sleeve cap has a slight amount of ease. By using the sewing machine's capabilities, that fullness can be effectively eased to fit the armhole. You'll master this technique in no time flat.

1 Do not join the underarm seams of the garment or the sleeve.

2 Easing is unnecessary. Pin the sleeve to the armhole with right sides together, meeting the cut edges, shoulder positions, and notches. Pin from the garment side.

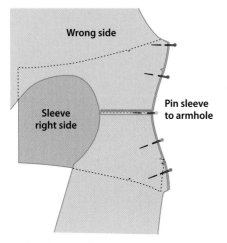

3 Position the sleeve and garment at the machine so the sleeve is next to the feed dogs.

Motivating Memo Whenever you join two pieces of fabric that are different lengths, always place the longer edge next to the sewing machine feed dogs. The feed dogs will ease the longer layer to meet the top layer.

4 Stitch the sleeve in place. Press the seams flat, then toward the sleeve.

5 Stitch the underarm seam, sewing both the side seam and sleeve underarm seam. Press the seam flat, then toward the back.

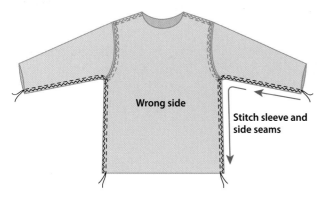

Cap Sleeve Construction

Sleeve ease is essential for wearing comfort, but it's also important that the sleeve fits smoothly into the armhole. If your garment has a cap sleeve with greater slope and a higher cap, this fullness must be eased to fit the armhole.

Easing Does It! – Sleeve Easing

Here are two options for easing in sleeve fullness. Experiment with these choices to see which you prefer. You want to get the best results in the least amount of time.

Option #1 - Sew two rows of machine stitching.
- Change the stitch length to basting, about six stitches per inch.
- Stitch one row of basting from notch to notch 5⁄8" from the cut edge of the sleeve cap. Leave 2" to 3" thread tails at the beginning and end of the stitching.
- Stitch a second basting row from notch to notch ¼" from the cut edge of the sleeve cap.

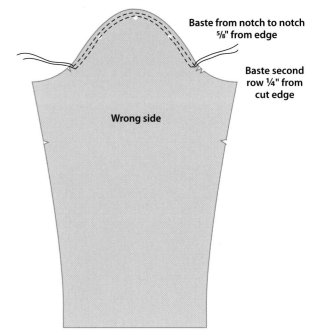

- Fasten the bobbin threads at one end of the stitching by wrapping them around a pin in a figure 8.

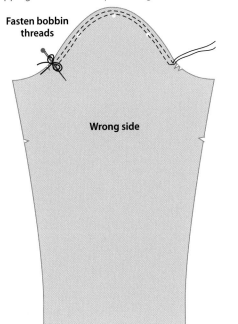

Fasten bobbin threads

Wrong side

- At the other end of the stitching, pull both bobbin threads until the size of the sleeve matches that of the armhole.
- Fasten the threads by wrapping them around a pin in a figure 8.

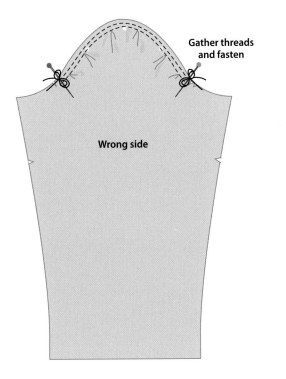

Gather threads and fasten

Wrong side

Option #2 - Finger easing.

This method requires only one row of stitching between notches and is perfect for lightweight to medium weight fabrics. If you haven't tried this technique before, practice on a fabric scrap until you get the hang of it.

- Adjust the stitch length according to the fabric weight: 10 to 12 stitches per inch for medium weight fabrics and 12 to 14 for lightweight.
- Stitch ½" from the cut edge of the sleeve cap.
- Firmly press your finger against the back of the presser foot. Stitch 2" to 3", trying to stop the fabric from flowing through the machine. Release your finger and repeat. Your finger will prevent the flow of fabric from behind the presser foot, causing the feed dogs to ease each stitch slightly.

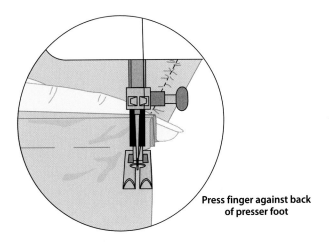

Press finger against back of presser foot

Motivating Memo It's important that you press very firmly. If you don't, the fabric will continue to move through the machine and the sleeve cap will not be eased. Press down hard with your finger.

- If you have eased too much, simply snip a stitch or two to release some of the gathers. If you need to gather more, pull a thread.

Setting in Cap Sleeves

After easing in the sleeve fullness, the next step is to insert the sleeve into the garment. Follow these streamlined steps for confidence-building results.

1 Stitch the shoulder and underarm seams of the front and back.
  • Match the cut edges and notches with right sides together and stitch the seam.
  • Press the seams flat, then open.

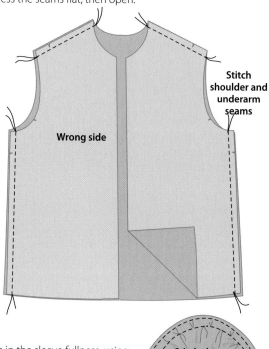

Stitch shoulder and underarm seams

Wrong side

2 Ease in the sleeve fullness, using one of the options detailed on pages 80-81.

3 Stitch the sleeve underarm seams. Press the seams flat, then open.

4 Turn the sleeve right side out. Insert the sleeve into the armhole with right sides together.

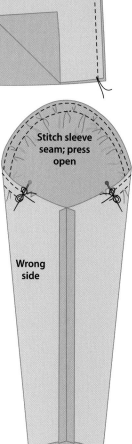

Stitch sleeve seam; press open

Wrong side

5 Pin the sleeve cap to the armhole, positioning the pin heads toward the cut edge. Distribute the ease evenly in the armhole, matching and pinning at these points:
  • Front and back notches
  • Underarm seam
  • Cap dot to shoulder seam

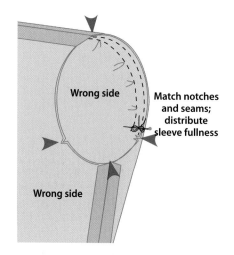

Wrong side

Match notches and seams; distribute sleeve fullness

Wrong side

6 Stitch the sleeve to the armhole.
  • Begin stitching at the notch to the right of the underarm seam, sewing with the sleeve on top to control the distribution of the fabric.
  • Stitch as far as the notch to the left of the armhole seam. Reposition the fabric; hold the fabric at a slight angle, allowing the feed dogs to "bite" or ease the longer sleeve to the shorter armhole. Stitch the remainder of the seam.

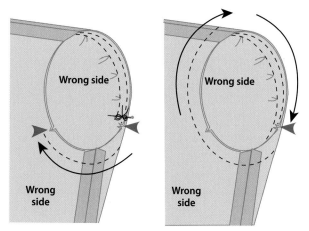

Wrong side

Wrong side

Wrong side

Wrong side

Stitch from notch to notch; reposition; stitch remainder

• When you reach the starting point, continue stitching until you reach the notch to the left of the underarm seam, sewing approximately ¼" from the first stitching to reinforce the underarm area.

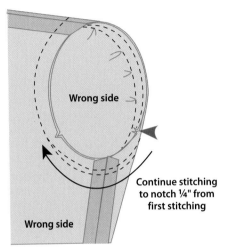

Wrong side

Wrong side

Continue stitching to notch ¼" from first stitching

• Trim the underarm between the notches to the second stitching. Zigzag or serge the underarm area to reinforce the stitching and to make the sleeve fit better.

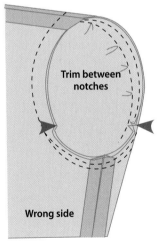

Trim between notches

Wrong side

7 Press the armhole seam for a smoother appearance.
• Press the seam flat, but don't press it open.
• Press all the seam allowances toward the sleeve, away from the garment. To help build shape into the sleeve, press it over a dressmaker's ham. The ham is shaped and curved like the armhole.
• Always press on the wrong side.

Nugget of Inspiration

When you're out on the dance floor, you don't want to have two left feet. The same thing applies in your sewing room. When you're making a top or jacket, you don't want to have two left sleeves! When setting in the sleeves, pay careful attention that you get a right and a left sleeve, and that they're each inserted on the correct side. The notches are different on the front and back of the sleeve for a reason!

CHAPTER 7

Finishing touches allow you to add your creative signature to a project. More than symbols of completion, finishing touches embody both an ending and a beginning, for even as you sew the final stitch of a project, breathing a bittersweet sigh of relief, your gaze shifts forward to envision future projects looming on the horizon.

Finishing Touches

...

Zippers

Don't avoid patterns that have zipper openings. Zippers may seem intimidating at first but if you follow these simplified steps, you'll find that their bark is worse than their bite. Who knows, you may even decide that inserting zippers is fun!

Getting Ready

1 Purchase a zipper about 2" longer than the pattern recommends. With the longer length, you won't have trouble stitching around the bulky zipper pull.

2 Decide whether you will use a centered zipper or a lapped zipper. Follow the directions for the one you choose.

3 Attach a zipper foot. Your zipper foot may not look exactly like the one pictured. Check your machine instruction manual if you need help identifying the foot.

Centered Zipper

A centered zipper is easy to insert. Two lines of straight stitching show on the right side of the fabric. The finished zipper has a sporty look. A centered zipper is preferred at center front openings and is sometimes used at back openings.

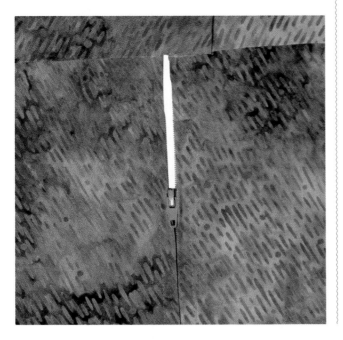

1 Baste the zipper opening with right sides together. Permanently stitch the rest of the seam and press the seam open.

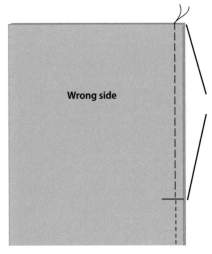

Wrong side

2 Center the zipper over the pressed seam allowance. Put the right side of the zipper next to the seam allowance. The lower edge of the zipper teeth should be at the end of the zipper opening. The pull tab will extend past the top of the fabric.

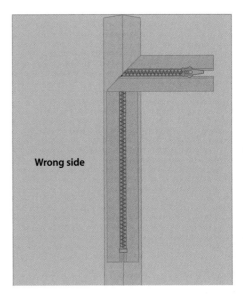

Wrong side

❸ Use strips of ½" wide tape such as Sewer's Fix-it Tape to hold the zipper to the seam allowance. Tape the top and bottom of the zipper. Add one or two more tape strips in the middle of the zipper, depending on the zipper's length.

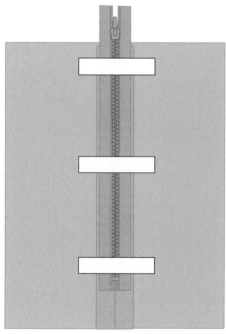

Tape zipper in place

❹ Turn the project right side out. Center another piece of ½" tape over the zipper seamline. The same amount of tape should extend on each side of the seam.

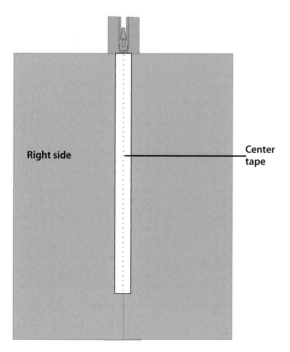

❺ Stitch across the bottom and up one side of the zipper, following the edge of the tape as a guide.

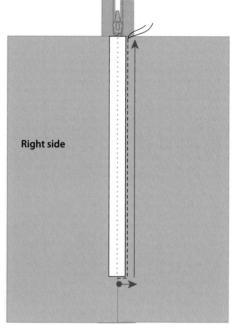

Stitch across bottom and up one side

❻ Repeat, stitching across the bottom and up the other side of the zipper. You may have to reposition the zipper foot or adjust the needle position. Check your machine instruction manual if you need help.

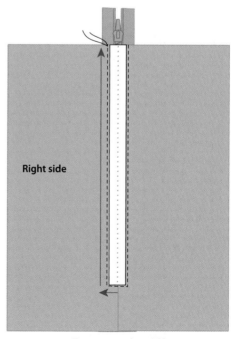

Repeat on other side

7 Remove the tape on the outside and inside of the project. Remove the basting stitches.

8 Pull the zipper tab down within the zipper opening. Set the stitch length to 0. Zigzag several times (bartack) across the upper ends of the zipper teeth so the pull won't come off. The extra zipper tape can be cut off after the top of the opening is finished with a facing or waistband.

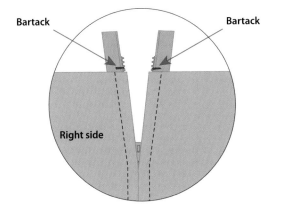

Lapped Zipper

A lapped zipper gives a tailored look. Only one line of stitching shows on the right side of the fabric. It's easier to keep the stitching straight and to make sure the zipper teeth are completely covered. The lapped zipper is preferred for side openings and is often used for back openings.

1 Before cutting out your garment, increase the zipper seam allowance to 1". For example, if the pattern allows a ⅝" seam allowance, add ⅜" to the seam in the zipper area.

2 Mark the 1" seamline at the top of the zipper opening on both the left and right seam allowances. These markings are very important.

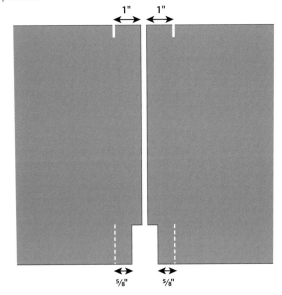

3 Stitch the seam below the zipper opening, stopping at the dot that marks the zipper opening and its wider seam allowance. Lock your stitches at the dot by sewing in place several times with the machine's stitch length set at 0.

4 Press the seam.
- Press the seam open below the zipper opening.
- On the garment's left side, fold and press under the entire 1" seam allowance in the zipper area. Use the marking and the lower end of the zipper opening to position the fold line.
- On the garment's right side, press under ⅞" of the 1" seam allowance to create the zipper underlay. The finished zipper will lap left over right.

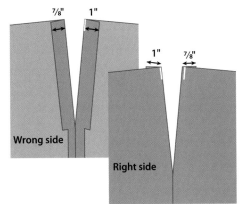

5 Insert the zipper.

- With right sides up, position the closed zipper under the zipper underlay with the bottom of the zipper at the base of the zipper opening. Place the underlay fold next to the right side of the zipper teeth. Make certain the zipper tab extends above the top of the garment. With short zippers, you shouldn't have to pin the zipper; you can merely finger pin and stitch.
- Position your machine's zipper foot to the left of the needle. Stitch next to the fold, from the bottom to the top.

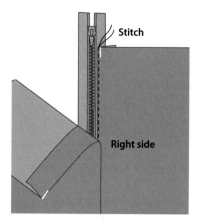

- Lap the left side of the garment over its right side, matching the markings. Tape the overlap in place.

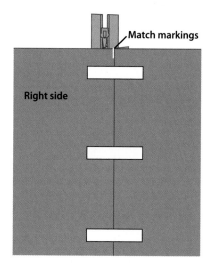

Tape overlap in place

Motivating Memo Pins sometimes create dimples in the fabric, causing uneven stitching. Instead of pins, use strips of Sewer's Fix-it Tape about 4" apart to position the lap. This ½" wide tape keeps the edge perfectly flat and results in a more even topstitching. When you're finished, you can easily remove the tape, leaving no sticky residue.

5 Topstitch the overlap.

- Align a strip of ½" wide Sewer's Fix-it Tape or transparent tape along the folded edge of the lapped seam allowance. This provides an accurate stitching guide.
- Slide the zipper foot to the right of the needle.
- Beginning at the base of the zipper, topstitch along the bottom edge of the tape and up the side.

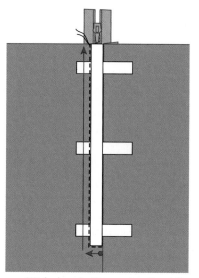

Stitch along bottom and up the side

- Remove the tape.

6 Complete the zipper insertion.

- Move the zipper pull down into the completed zipper placket. Satin stitch or bartack over the ends of the zipper tape at the top of the zipper for reinforcement.
- Cut off the excess zipper tape.

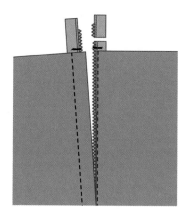

Invisible Zipper

An invisible zipper is a special type of zipper designed to look like a garment seam when closed. You can insert an invisible zipper in side, center back, or center front seams. **Note:** *The following instructions are for a center back opening. They can easily be adapted for other openings.*

1 Prepare the zipper opening and the facing.
- Do not stitch the seam closed. The entire seam remains open during zipper insertion.
- Mark the ⅝" seam allowances for the zipper opening on the right side of both garment sections. This identifies where to position the zipper teeth during zipper application.

⅝"

Motivating Memo Most tape measures are ⅝" wide, so you can easily transfer that marking by simply placing the edge of a tape measure along the fabric's cut edge. Then mark along the opposite edge of the tape measure using a water-soluble marking pen or chalk.

• Trim ⅝" from the center back of both facings. A smaller facing later causes the garment seam allowance to wrap around the zipper.

Trim ⅝" from facing

⅝"

2 Insert the invisible zipper.
- Press the zipper to flatten the zipper coils. Doing so makes insertion easier. One word of caution: Use a cool temperature setting. Since the coils are usually made of nylon or polyester, too much heat can damage them.
- Attach a zipper roller foot. The roller on this special foot allows it to glide over the fabric and zipper. The foot is also hinged to permit smooth stitching over bulky fabrics and crossed seams.
- Open the zipper. With right sides together, place the zipper so one tape edge is even with the edge of one back seam allowance, and the zipper teeth are at the marked seamline.

Marked seamline

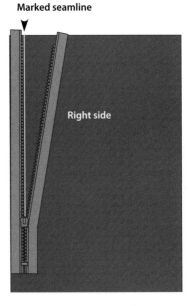

Right side

- Stitch next to the zipper teeth from top to bottom. You will not be able to stitch completely to the bottom of the zipper; a short section remains unstitched.

- Close the zipper. Pin the unstitched side of the zipper to the remaining back seam allowance with right sides together. This ensures that the two sides of the garment will meet on the finished application. Open the zipper and stitch the second side of the zipper.

❸ Close the seam at the bottom of the zipper.
- Replace the roller foot with a conventional zipper foot.
- Reposition the zipper foot to the left of the needle.
- Meet the garment seam edges below the zipper with right sides together. Stitch the seam, overlapping a few stitches at the bottom of the zipper.

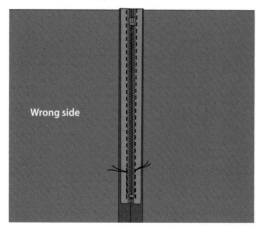

❹ Attach the facing.
- Stitch the front facing to the back facing at the shoulder seams with right sides together.

- Pin the facing to the garment at the center back with right sides together. Stitch a ¼" seam at each center back edge.

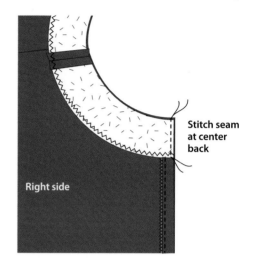

- Meet the facing to the neckline with right sides together, matching the shoulder seams. Pin. Since the facing is smaller than the garment, the garment wraps around the zipper, with the zipper teeth at the fold.
- Stitch the neckline seam.

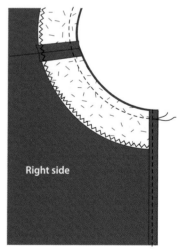

- Grade and trim the seam. Understitch the seam allowances.
- Turn the facing to the wrong side.

Exposed Zipper

This is an extremely easy method for inserting a zipper. It's especially useful for making bags. If you're using fabrics that don't ravel, such as oilcloth, you don't even need to finish the edges. How's that for easy!

1 If necessary, finish the seam edges by serging or zigzagging to prevent raveling.

2 Position the zipper along one finished edge, meeting the wrong side of the zipper to the right side of the fabric. Make sure that the fabric is a scant ¼" away from the zipper teeth to allow room for opening and closing the zipper. Stitch.

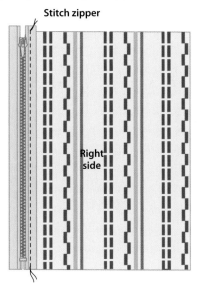

Stitch zipper

Right side

3 Add a second line of stitching close to the first stitching to reinforce the zipper.

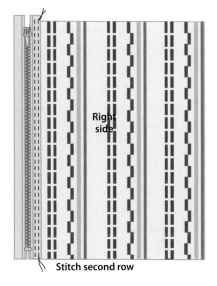

Right side

Stitch second row

4 Repeat, stitching the zipper to the opposite edge of the fabric as detailed above.

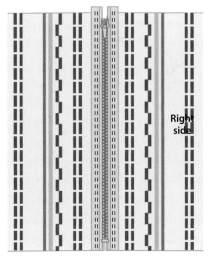

Right side

Stitch zipper to opposite edge

Hems

Nearly everything you sew has a hem – skirts, pants, sleeves; even home décor items such as curtains and table linens. By using a few simple hints, you can turn this time-consuming chore into a simple sewing task.

- Prepress the hem on each flat piece before stitching it to another piece. This is a great timesaving technique, especially when you're sewing children's sleeves, gift bag casings, or any circular area that's hard to press.
- Use an Ezy-Hem Gauge to provide an accurate measurement and to avoid leaving a hem impression on the right side of the fabric. Place the gauge on the wrong side of the fabric. Fold up the hem allowances over the gauge to the desired width and press.

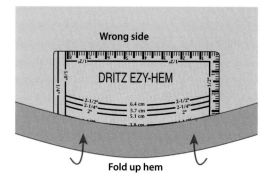
Wrong side
DRITZ EZY-HEM
Fold up hem

Nugget of Inspiration

Although thread is considered the "proper" material for securing a hem, in a pinch many of us have been known to substitute other, less desirable options. Admit it, there are times when you've noticed that the hem of your pants was coming loose and reached for the stapler or tape dispenser to remedy the problem. The important thing to remember is that you're not the only one who does these things. You may be one of the few who will admit it, but lots of people do it.

Easy Hems

Preparing a hem for stitching is a simple three-step process. Then you can choose from several different ways of securing the hem.

❶ After stitching the side seams, press the hem at the seam areas. Grade the seam allowances within the hem area to reduce bulk.

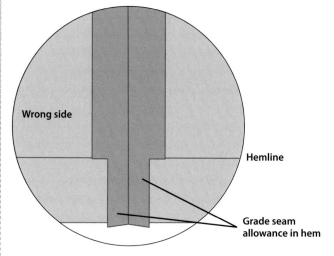
Wrong side
Hemline
Grade seam allowance in hem

❷ Finish the cut edge of the hem by zigzagging, serging, or clean finishing the edges. (See page 64 for more details.)

❸ Fold up the hem along the prepressed hemline and pin it in place.

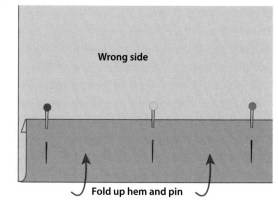
Wrong side
Fold up hem and pin

❹ Secure the hem in one of the following ways:
- Topstitch the hem in place. To topstitch, straight stitch on the right side of the fabric, parallel to the hem edge, approximately ⅜" from the hem edge, or your desired distance from the hem edge.

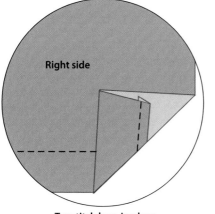

Topstitch hem in place

- Hand stitch the hem in place using a blind hem stitch.
  - Thread a needle with a single strand of thread. Cut the thread about 18" long. The thread will tangle and knot more easily if it is too long.
  - Knot one end of the thread.
  - Fold back the project edge so about ¼" of the hem edge shows.

Fold back hem so ¼" shows

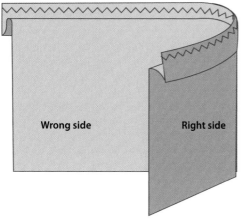

- Work from right to left.
- Take a tiny stitch in the hem; then take a tiny stitch in the project about ¼" ahead of that stitch. Pick up only one or two threads in the fabric.

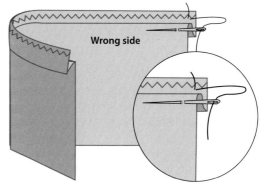

- Take a stitch in the hem edge about 1/4" ahead of the last stitch.
- Repeat, alternating stitches between the hem edge and the project.

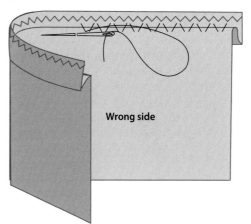

- Don't pull the stitches too tight or the hem will pucker.

Nugget of Inspiration

One of the best things about hand sewing is that you can do it on the couch while watching television. Be careful, though, that you don't sew through the clothing you're wearing. I know you're laughing, but it's easy to do. And when you stand up, your newly hemmed item will be hanging from your clothing like a dryer sheet. A good idea is to place a book or lap desk on your lap to prevent this "sticky" predicament.

• Stitch the hem using a machine blind hem stitch.
  - Fold back the project edge so about ¼" of the hem edge shows.

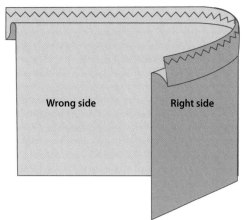

Wrong side   Right side

  - Adjust your sewing machine for a blind hem stitch as detailed in your owner's manual.
  - Stitch so the straight stitch falls in the hem allowance and the zigzag just catches the project at the fold.

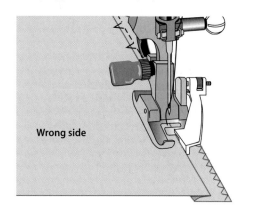

Wrong side

Nugget of Inspiration

The hem area is an ideal place to add some unique touches. You might stitch the hem using one of your machine's decorative stitches or with a contrasting thread color.

Decorative stitch

Fused Hems

Fusing is a fast and easy way to finish a hem. You can hem your project with a fusible web and the heat of an iron. Hemming it will be fast, and it doesn't require any hand sewing. Fusing works best on knits and lightweight wovens.

Motivating Memo Make a quick test sample and try the fusible web on a fabric scrap to see if this is the hem finish you want to use on your project.

Be careful when you fuse hems. Once the web melts, it's permanent. You have only one chance to get it right. **Note:** *Don't use this hemming method if you may need to alter the hem length (often necessary in children's clothes).*
Use one of the following methods to fuse hems:

Unbacked Fusible Web (Such as Fine Fuse)
❶ Place a strip of ½" to ¾" wide fusible web along the wrong side of the hem edge.

❷ Serge or zigzag the fusible web in place. Trim any web that extends past the edge.

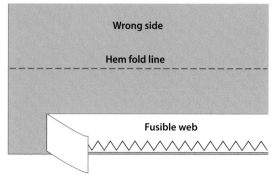

Wrong side

Hem fold line

Fusible web

❸ Fold up the hem. Measure so the entire hem is the same width. Pin.

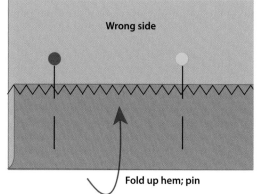

Wrong side

Fold up hem; pin

❹ Cover the hem with a damp press cloth. Press with a steam iron to fuse the hem to the project.

Paper-Backed Fusible Web (Such as Wonder-Under)

1 Finish the raw edge by zigzagging or serging.

2 Cut ½" to ¾" wide strips of paper-backed fusible web.

3 Position the web side on the wrong side of the hem, paper side up, placing the web ¼" above the hem edge. Press.

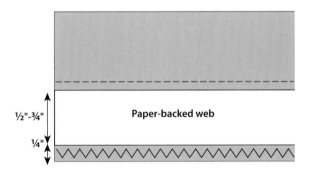

½"-¾"

¼"

Paper-backed web

4 Remove the paper backing.

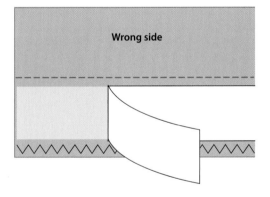

Wrong side

5 Fold up the hem; measure so the entire hem is the same width. Fuse.

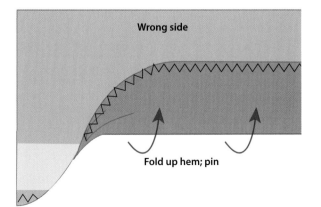

Wrong side

Fold up hem; pin

Double Needle Hems for Knits

A double needle hem retains stretch, or give, in the crosswise grain, making it ideal for knit fabrics. ***Note:*** *Double needles only fit zigzag machines that thread from front to back.*

1 Press up the hem.

2 Replace your sewing machine needle with a double needle.

Motivating Memo When sewing with a double needle, thread the top of the machine with two spools, placing them so they unwind in opposite directions. Thread the machine as if the two were a single thread, separating them at the needles.

3 Working from the right side of the garment, stitch an even distance from the hem fold. When you finish, the right side of the garment will have two equidistant rows of stitching and zigzag stitching will appear on the wrong side, since the bobbin thread moves back and forth between the two needle threads.

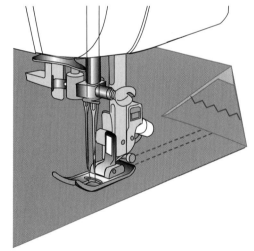

4 Trim any hem allowance that extends beyond the stitching on the wrong side of the fabric.

Nugget of Inspiration

If most of the pants you buy drag on the floor, you now have the skills to fix that problem. Since you are now a master hemmer, you can quickly do this simple alteration on purchased pants or skirts. And while wearing high heels is a lot of fun, you shouldn't be forced to wear them just because your pants are too long.

Closures

They may be small, but closures play a very important role as the things that hold your projects together. And while closures are generally thought of in terms of clothing, they also appear quite frequently in home décor projects. Think about your favorite shirt, coat, pillow, or other item with buttons or snaps; you might not notice the buttons or snaps all the time, but if one should fall off, you definitely take notice. Obviously, these little things deserve some attention. Choose from the following options to keep your projects together.

Buttonholes

❶ Check your instruction manual to see how your machine makes buttonholes. Some machines have built-in buttonholers, while others use special attachments. Always make a test buttonhole on a fabric scrap before working on your project.

Motivating Memo When making your test buttonhole, stitch on the same grain of the fabric as on your project. If the project buttonholes follow the lengthwise grain, use that grain for your test buttonhole. If the buttonholes follow the crosswise grain, stitch the buttonhole along that grain. Include a layer of interfacing between the fabric layers so the test buttonhole is exactly like it will be in your project.

❷ Mark the buttonhole positions.
- On garments, horizontal buttonholes should end ⅛" past the project's center front or center back. Vertical buttonholes should be exactly on the center line.

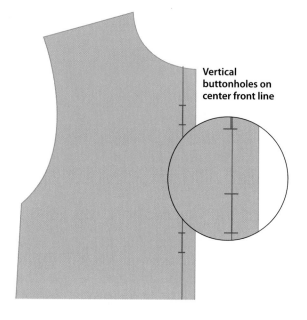

Vertical buttonholes on center front line

- Buttonholes should be equal distances apart. If you altered your pattern, you may need to respace the buttonholes.
- Transfer the buttonhole positions from your pattern to your project with a washable marking pen or a chalk line.

❸ Determine the buttonhole length.
- Measure the length and thickness of the button.
  - Place a piece of string or tape around the button. Place the button on a flat surface. Start measuring at the bottom edge of the button, go across the top, and stop at the opposite bottom edge. Mark the starting and stopping points on the tape or string.

Mark starting and stopping points

  - Measure the length of the tape between the marks. This tells you how long the buttonhole should be.

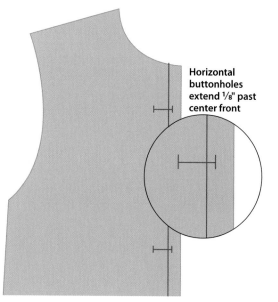

Horizontal buttonholes extend ⅛" past center front

- At each buttonhole marking, measure the buttonhole length. Mark both ends.

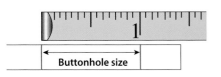

Buttonhole size

- Place strips of tape at the buttonhole ends to provide guides for starting and stopping stitching.

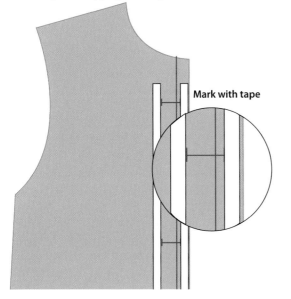

Mark with tape

4 Stitch the buttonholes.
- Place a layer of interfacing between the buttonholes and the facing. If the pattern does not include interfacing, place a strip of interfacing slightly wider and longer than the buttonholes between the two layers of fabric.

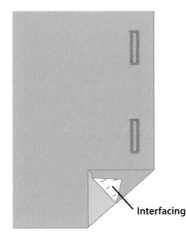

Interfacing

- Stitch the buttonholes, following the directions in your instruction manual.

5 Open the buttonhole using one of the following methods:

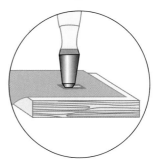

- Use a buttonhole cutter and block.
- Use a seam ripper. To prevent cutting past the bartacks at each end of the buttonhole, place a pin across each end.

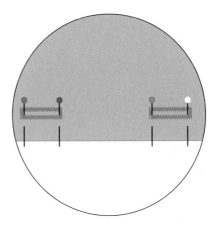

Hand-Sewn Buttons

Each button must have a shank so there is room for the buttonhole to fit under the button. A shank is a plastic or metal extension under the button and is found on buttons without holes.

Buttons with holes do not have shanks; you must add thread shanks.

Shank

1 Mark the button position directly under the buttonhole. Place the button over the mark.

2 Use a doubled, knotted thread. Hide the knot between the fabric and the button.

3 Put a small knitting needle, a round toothpick, or a large darning needle on top of the button between the button's holes.

4 Sew five or six stitches through the holes, stitching over the needle or toothpick.

5 Bring the threaded needle up from the underside of the project between the button and the fabric.

6 Remove the toothpick or needle. Pull the button to the top of the threads.

7 Wind the needle thread tightly around the threads between the button and the fabric five or six times, forming a shank.

8 Bring the threaded needle back to the underside of the fabric. Knot the thread close to the fabric.

Motivating Memo To sew on a button with a shank, position the shank on the marked button position. Use a doubled, knotted thread to sew five or six stitches through the shank. Bring the threaded needle back to the underside as directed above and knot the thread close to the fabric.

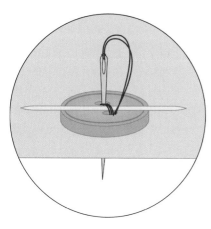

Stitch button to garment, stitching over toothpick

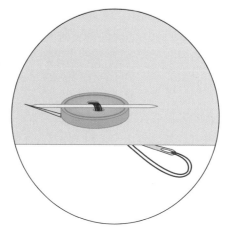

Bring needle up from underside between button and fabric

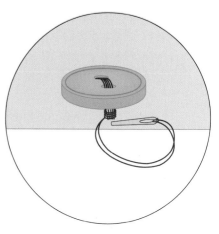

Bring threaded needle back to underside; knot

Machine-Sewn Buttons

Use your sewing machine's fringe foot, tailor tack foot, or button foot to sew on buttons. The foot's high center bar helps create the shank for the button.

Motivating Memo If you're sewing a button on a project that's likely to see a lot of stress – a child's garment, athletic item, or tote bag, for example – use two strands of all-purpose thread. After sewing, apply a drop of seam sealant such as Fray Check.

❶ Attach the fringe, tailor tack, or button foot.

❷ Use Sewer's Fix-it Tape or transparent tape to position your button on the project. Position the tape on the button so you won't stitch through it.

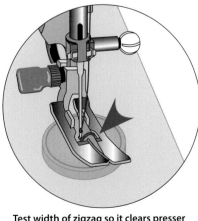

Position tape so needle won't go through it

❸ Set your machine in the position for bartacking (zigzag with 0 stitch length). Turn the wheel by hand several times to check the correct zigzag width for your buttons.

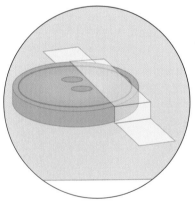

Test width of zigzag so it clears presser foot extension

❹ Zigzag five or six times. Lock the stitches by setting the stitch width to 0 and stitching several times in the left needle position. Cut your threads, leaving 10" to 12" tails.

❺ Stitch the remaining buttons in the same manner. Remove the tape.

❻ Form thread shanks.
- Pull each button up so that the excess thread forms a shank between the button and the fabric.
- Thread a needle with the needle thread tail. Bring the needle thread to the wrong side of the fabric.
- Thread the needle with both thread tails. Pull the thread tails through the fabric so they meet at the shank.
- Tightly wrap the tails around the shank five or six times.

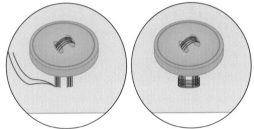

Wrap thread tails around thread shank

- Bring the threaded needle back to the underside of the fabric. Knot the thread close to the fabric.

Nugget of Inspiration
Choose buttons that express your personality and reflect the style of the project. Don't be tempted to be safe with buttons that merely blend in with their background. Instead, go out of your way to find unique buttons that capture the spirit of the project. The buttons don't have to scream out, "Notice Me!" You can achieve a subtle effect that is still breathtaking. It all depends on your personality and the nature of your project.

Snaps

Use snaps to hold together edges that overlap and don't get much strain. Snaps come in several sizes, ranging from a tiny size 4/0 to a large size 4.

Attach the ball half of the snap to the wrong side of the overlap and the socket half to the right side of the underlap.

1 Sew on the ball half first.
- Use a single, knotted thread. Hide the knot between the fabric and the snap.
- Stitch through one hole several times, placing the stitches close together. Stitch only through the facing and the interfacing. *Do not* stitch through to the right side of the project.

Stitch only through facing

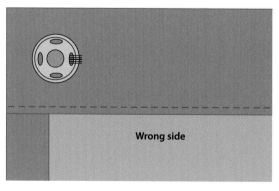

Wrong side

- After stitching one hole, insert the needle under the snap. Bring the thread out in the next hole.

Insert needle under snap; bring thread out in next hole

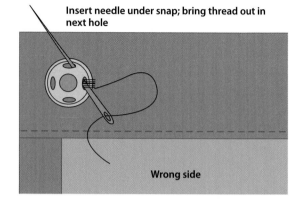

Wrong side

- Stitch through all four holes in the same way. Knot the thread close to the fabric.

Motivating Memo To mark the location for the socket quickly and easily, rub a piece of chalk over the end of the ball. Position the ball over the other part of the project as if the project was closed. Finger press the two fabric layers together. The chalk will mark the position for the socket.

Rub ball with chalk; press to mark

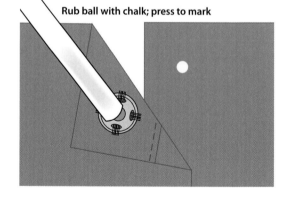

2 Position the socket half on the fabric and stitch through the socket holes just as you stitched through those on the ball half.

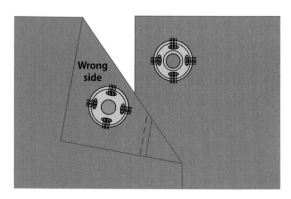

Wrong side

Swing/Hanging Snaps

Snaps can also hold together two edges that meet, preventing them from gaping or pulling apart. These snaps are called swing or hanging snaps.

❶ Place the ball half of the snap at one edge of the opening so that only one hole touches the fabric. The remainder of the ball will extend past the fabric edge.

❷ Stitch the ball half to the garment, sewing through only one hole. Use a single, knotted thread.

Back of ball half

Wrong side

❸ Rub chalk on the ball. Place the two project sections so the edges of the opening just meet. Mark the position for the socket half.

Mark position with chalk

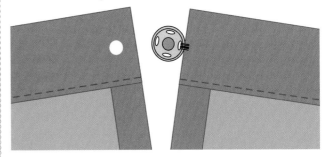

❹ Stitch through all the holes of the socket half, sewing through only the facing and interfacing.

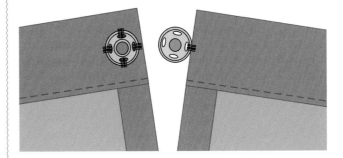

Hooks and Eyes

Use hooks and eyes to fasten openings where there will be greater stress, such as on waistbands. Use a straight eye when the edges overlap and a looped eye when the edges only meet. Regular hooks and eyes are available in sizes 0 through 3, with 3 being the largest.

1 Sew on the hook.
- Place the hook on the overlap, with its end (the bill) about ⅛" from the edge.
- Use a single, knotted thread. Fasten the thread under the hook.
- Stitch around both rings, placing the stitches close together. Stitch through only the facing and interfacing. *Do not* stitch through to the right side of the garment.

Sew on rings, stitching only through facing

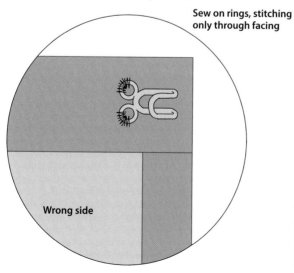

Wrong side

- Before fastening the thread, fasten the bill with several overhand stitches. This helps keep the top layer flat when the hook is fastened. Stitch over only the lower part of the bill, rather than over both parts.

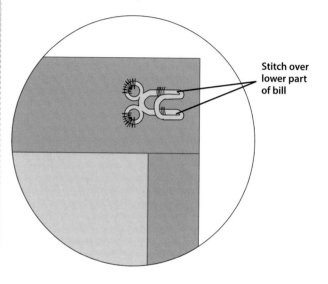

Stitch over lower part of bill

2 Sew on the eye.
- Position the hook over the other part of the garment as if it were fastened.
- Place the straight eye or the loop of the rounded eye directly under the hook. Mark its position.
- Stitch around the rings of the eye.

Hook and Loop Tape

Hook and loop tape, such as Velcro or Fix Velour, is especially useful for children and adults who have difficulty fastening and opening buttons and other closures. It's also an extremely easy closure to work with, making it an attractive option regardless of where you apply it.

Motivating Memo Here's a hint from one of my viewers. When sewing the hook side of hook and loop tape, the thread sometimes catches on the hooks. To remedy this, place a small piece of water-soluble stabilizer over the hook tape while stitching. Use a seam ripper to remove the stabilizer when you're done stitching.

❶ Position the hook side of the hook and loop tape on one section of your project. Stitch the outer edges in place.

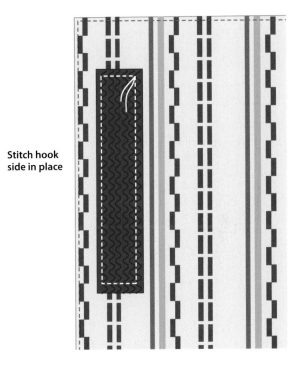

Stitch hook side in place

❷ Position the loop side of the hook and loop tape in the corresponding position on the second section and stitch in place.

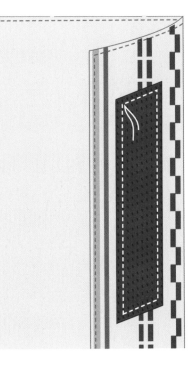

Stitch loop side in place

Patch Pockets

Patch pockets are great additions not only to garments, but also to other projects such as tote bags and pillows. Extremely versatile, they're also quite easy to construct. Even if your pattern doesn't include pockets, it's easy to add them using this technique.

Nugget of Inspiration

Try using pockets in unexpected ways. For example, add some pockets to sheer curtains and put dried herbs or colorful stones in the pockets. Use this idea to add interest to a shower curtain as well.

Patch Pocket Basics

Patch pockets can range from basic squares with pointed corners to squares with rounded corners. Regardless of their form, shaping these pockets involves only a few basic steps.

Preparing the Pocket

1 Mark the pocket by making ¼" nips at the pocket hemline to indicate the fold line.

2 Mark the pocket position on the project using a fabric marking pen.

3 Interface the pocket.
- Cut a strip of interfacing the size of the pocket hem.
- Fuse the interfacing to the wrong side of the pocket hem, following the manufacturer's instructions.

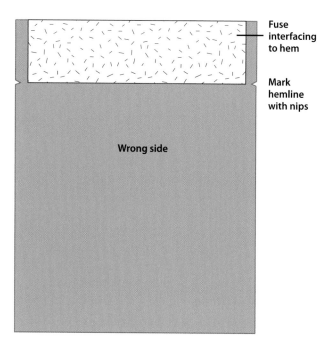

Fuse interfacing to hem

Mark hemline with nips

Wrong side

Motivating Memo On some fabrics (such as knits) you may want to cut the interfacing the size of the completed pocket to interface the entire pocket.

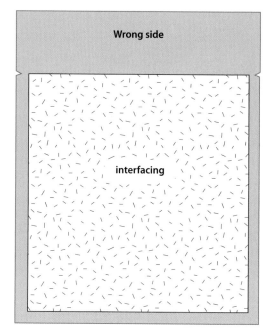

Wrong side

interfacing

4 Finish the edge of the pocket hem by zigzagging, serging, or turning under the edge and stitching.

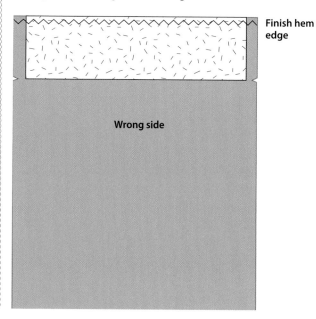

Finish hem edge

Wrong side

5 Fold the hem to the outside of the pocket along the fold line.

6 Stitch the side seams on the hem.

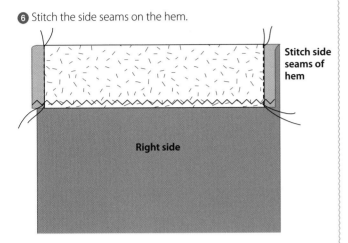

Stitch side
seams of
hem

Right side

7 Grade the seam allowances. Trim the pocket allowance to ⅜"
and the hem allowance to ¼". Trim the upper corners diagonally.

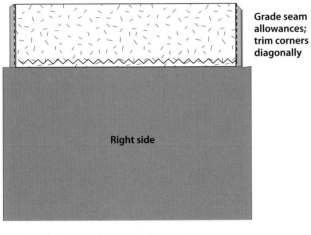

Grade seam
allowances;
trim corners
diagonally

Right side

8 Turn the hem to the inside of the pocket.

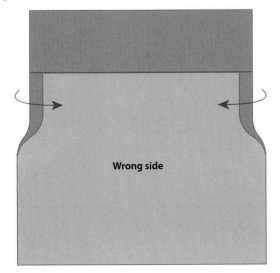

Wrong side

Shaping Pockets with Square Corners

1 Miter the corners.
  • Measure and mark 1¼" from either side of one lower pocket
    corner.

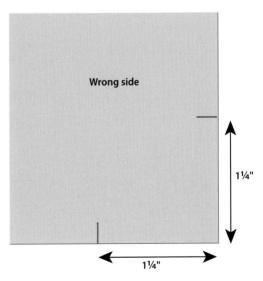

Wrong side

1¼"

1¼"

- Place a strip of tape on the wrong side of the fabric between the two marks, extending the tape ends.

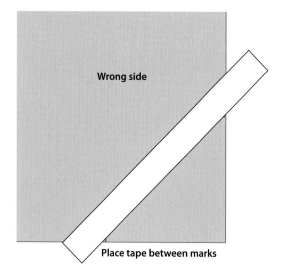

Place tape between marks

- With right sides together, fold the corner to a point, aligning the marks and the tape.
- Stitch next to, but not through, the tape to form the miter.

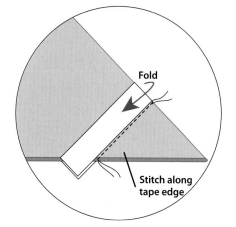

Fold

Stitch along tape edge

- Remove the tape and trim the seam to ¼".

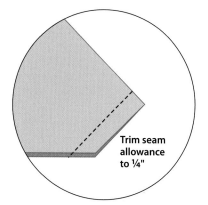

Trim seam allowance to ¼"

- Repeat for the second corner.
- Press the seams open.
- Turn the mitered corners right side out.

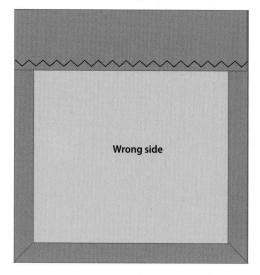

Wrong side

❷ Press the pocket.
- Press the side seam allowances to the wrong side, using the straight edge of an Ezy-Hem Gauge as a pressing guide. Place the gauge on the wrong side of the fabric. Fold the seam allowance on one side of the pocket over the gauge and press. Repeat for the other side of the pocket. The gauge acts as a buffer, eliminating seam show-through, and also serves as a measuring guide.

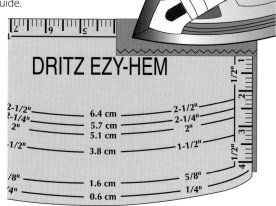

- Repeat this step on the lower edge of the pocket.

Motivating Memo Because the Ezy-Hem Gauge is metal, it gets very hot when you press over it. Let it cool for a few seconds before removing it from the pocket.

Shaping Pockets with Rounded Corners

1 Press the side and lower seam allowances like you did for the pocket with square corners, using an Ezy-Hem Gauge but stopping prior to the corner curve.

2 Use a Pocket Curve Template to shape the corner.
- Place one of the template's corner curves on the wrong side of the fabric along the pocket seamline. Align the straight sections of the template with the prepressed side and lower press marks.
- Mold the corner seam allowance over the template.
- Attach the clip section of the template to hold the seam allowance in place. Press. If necessary, trim excess seam allowances.

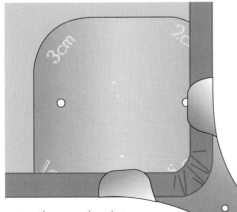

- Repeat on the second pocket corner.
- Press the hem edge as detailed for pockets with square corners.

Positioning and Stitching Pockets

1 Place the pocket on the right side of the project, matching the pocket top corners to the pocket position marks. Because stitching over pins sometimes causes uneven topstitching, use strips of Sewer's Fix-it Tape to hold the pocket in place.

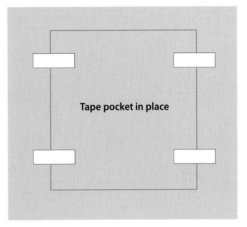

Tape pocket in place

2 Machine stitch the pocket to the project, stitching through the tape. Reinforce the upper corners by backstitching or stitching several stitches across the top edge on each side. Remove the tape when you've finished stitching.

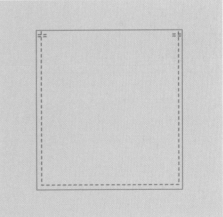

Nugget of Inspiration

Pockets are another great opportunity for adding a designer touch to a project. Why settle for basic square pockets when there are so many great shapes in the world? Experiment with abstract shapes or with specific ones such as fruit, coffee cups, or flowers. Choose a pocket that reflects the theme of the project, whether you're picking up shapes from the fabric print or choosing a shape based on the overall feel of the project. Whatever you do, don't be afraid to be creative!

CHAPTER 8

Expanding your vision is part of the natural progression of this journey. As you gain confidence in your skills, you begin to explore the world outside of the box. You may take baby steps at first, but soon you will be moving by leaps and bounds, stretching your imagination beyond the realm of self-inflicted limitation. Your fears dissolve as you embrace your inner seamstress and express that spirit in your creations.

Expanding Your Vision

Curtains

Life is too short to live in a space with bare windows. Curtains not only cover windows, they bring a room together, adding the finishing touches to your decorating scheme. To dress up windows and breathe new life into a room, stitch some curtains to add color, character, and cover. Whether you need curtains in the kitchen, bedroom, or living room, choose fabric to complement your décor and personal style for a look that's unique and totally you!

Basic Curtain

Basic Curtain Instructions

1 Cut the fabric.

- To determine the fabric dimensions, measure your window from outside edge to outside edge and top to bottom.
  - Decide if you want the curtain to be very full and gathered or more of a straight panel with little or no gathering.
  - Keep in mind that the position of the curtain rod will affect the length of the curtain.
  - The style of curtain will also affect the length. For example, the basic curtain is designed with a 1" header above the casing.
  - For curtains with tabs, the tabs add 1½", so you would add an additional 1½" to the length.

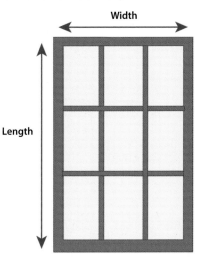

Width

Length

Motivating Memo If you want a very full curtain, you may need to double or even triple the width of the window to get the desired effect. If you're unsure, use a sheet or piece of fabric to experiment.

- Determine the dimensions of the finished curtain, then add seam allowances, hems, and casing to those measurements. For the basic curtain, add the following:
  - Add 6½" to the length (4" for the casing and header, 2½" for the lower hem).
  - Add 2" to the width for the side hems.

Motivating Memo If the fabric you're using doesn't ravel, or if you use the selvages as the sides of the curtain, you don't need to hem the sides. In that case, don't add the extra 2" to the width.

- For example, for a finished curtain measuring 40" wide x 42" long, add the following:
  - Width, 40" + 2" (side hems) = 42"
  - Length, 42" + 4" (casing and header) + 2½" (lower hem) = 48½"
- Cut your fabric according to these dimensions. In this example, you would cut a rectangle 42" x 48½".

2 Finish the sides.

- Turn under ½" along each side edge and press.
- Turn under another ½" and press.

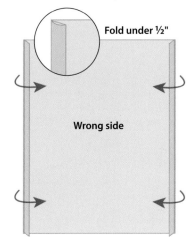

Fold under ½"

Wrong side

- Stitch close to each folded edge.

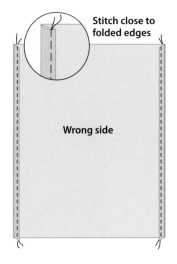

Stitch close to folded edges

Wrong side

3 Form the casing.
  • Turn under and press ½" along the top edge.

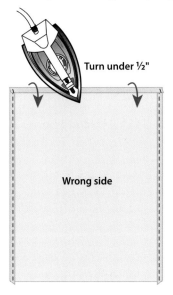

  • Turn under and press 2½" along the top edge.

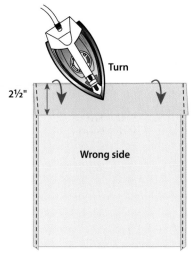

  • Stitch 1" from the top folded edge.
  • Stitch close to the bottom folded edge.

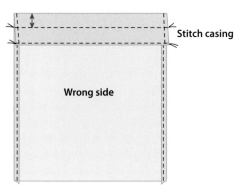

4 Hem the curtain.
  • Turn under ½" along the bottom edge and press.
  • Turn under 2" along the bottom edge and press.

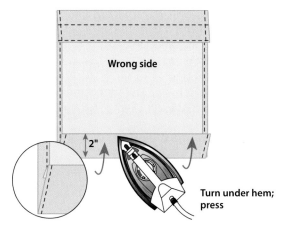

  • Stitch close to the top folded edge of the hem.

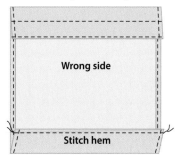

5 Insert the curtain rod into the casing, hang the curtain, and enjoy!

Variation 1: Curtain with Tabs

Variation 1: Curtain with Tabs Instructions

1 Determine the fabric dimensions as detailed in Step 1 for the Basic Curtain, adding the following:
- Add 2½" to the length; ½" for the casing; 2" for the lower hem.
- Add 2" to the width for the side hems.

Motivating Memo When determining the finished dimensions of the curtain, remember that the tabs will add 1½" to the length.

2 Cut the fabrics.
- Curtain: Cut the fabric according to your determined dimensions.
- Facing: Cut a rectangle 3" x the width of your curtain fabric.
- Tabs: Cut a 4" x 6" rectangle for each tab.

Motivating Memo The number of tabs you need depends on the width of your curtain and how far apart you space the tabs. For example, the finished width of the pictured curtain is 54". We used nine tabs and spaced them approximately 5" apart.

3 Finish the sides of the curtain as detailed in Step 2 for the Basic Curtain.

4 Prepare the tabs.
- Fold one 4" x 6" rectangle in half, meeting the lengthwise edges.
  - Stitch a ½" seam along the lengthwise edge.

Stitch

  - Turn the tab right side out, positioning the seam at one edge. Press.
  - Fold the tab in half, meeting the short edges. Press.
  - Repeat for each tab.

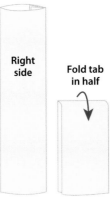

Right side

Fold tab in half

- Place the curtain on your work surface, right side up.
- Position the tabs on the right side of the curtain, aligning the cut edges and spacing them an equal distance apart. Machine baste the tabs in place.

Baste tabs in place

Right side

5 Prepare the facing.
- Turn under and press ½" on each 3" edge of the facing.

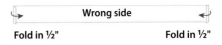

Wrong side

Fold in ½"   **Fold in ½"**

- Turn under and press ½" on the bottom edge of the facing.

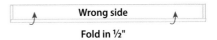

Wrong side

Fold in ½"

- Position the facing over the tabs with right sides together, meeting the cut edges.

Position facing

Wrong side

Right side

• Stitch, using a ½" seam.

Stitch facing to curtain

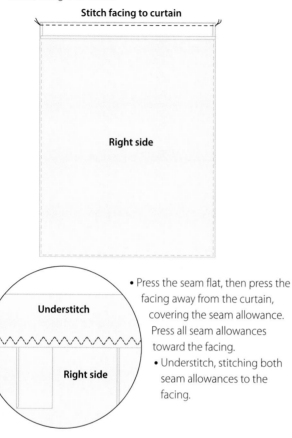

Right side

• Pin baste the sides of the facing in place.

• Press the seam flat, then press the facing away from the curtain, covering the seam allowance. Press all seam allowances toward the facing.

• Understitch, stitching both seam allowances to the facing.

Understitch

Right side

Motivating Memo Try using a multi-step zigzag for understitching. Instead of just zigzagging back and forth, the machine makes several stitches for each zig and zag. This helps the facing lie smooth. Check your instruction manual to see if your machine can sew this stitch.

• Turn the facing to the wrong side and press.

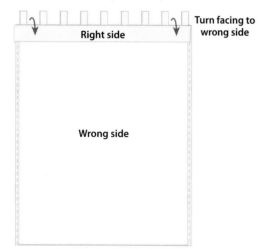

Right side

Turn facing to wrong side

Wrong side

• Stitch the facing to the curtain, stitching close to the folded edge.

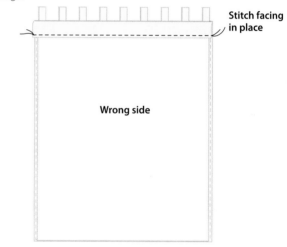

Stitch facing in place

Wrong side

• Hand stitch the sides of the facing.

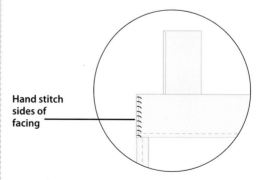

Hand stitch sides of facing

❻ Hem the curtain as detailed in Step 4 for the Basic Curtain.

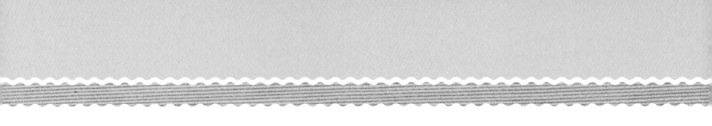

Variation 2: Sheer Curtain with Scalloped Hem

Variation 2: Sheer Curtain with Scalloped Hem Instructions

❶ Choose a fabric that is hemmed along one edge. We used a sheer decorator fabric with a scalloped hem along each selvage edge. When cutting out the fabric, make sure to cut with the selvage edge as the hem edge.

❷ Determine the fabric dimensions as detailed in Step 1 for the Basic Curtain, eliminating the extra length for the lower hem.

❸ Finish the sides and form the casing as detailed for the Basic Curtain.

Variation 3: Denim Curtain with Pockets

Variation 3: Denim Curtain with Pockets Instructions

Special Supplies
- Denim fabric
- 3 jeans back pockets
- Belt loops (we used 9)
- Jeans Stitch Thread

1 Cut the fabric.
- To determine the fabric dimensions, measure your window. Since this curtain is designed to be a flat panel, the finished width measurement should be close to the window width.
- Determine the dimensions of the finished curtain. Add seam allowances, hem, and casing to those measurements. For the denim curtain, add the following:
  - Add 3" to the length (2" for the casing, 1" for the lower hem).
  - Add 2" to the width for the side hems.
- For example, for a curtain with finished measurements of 12" long x 22" wide, the starting dimensions would be:
  - Length, 12" + 2" (casing) + 1" (lower hem) = 15"
  - Width, 22" + 2" (side hems) = 24"
- Cut your fabric according to these dimensions. In this example, you would cut a rectangle 15" x 24".
- Remove belt loops and pockets from old jeans.

Nugget of Inspiration
If you don't have a pair of jeans that are ready to be sacrificed, visit some thrift stores and second-hand shops. These are wonderful resources for finding inexpensive jeans.

2 Finish the sides.
- Turn under and press ½" along each side edge.

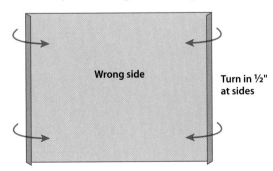

Turn in ½" at sides

Wrong side

- Turn under another ½" and press.
- Stitch close to each inside folded edge using Jeans Stitch Thread.

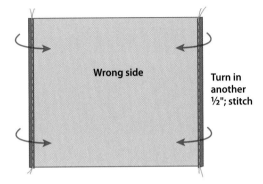

Wrong side

Turn in another ½"; stitch

- Add another line of topstitching halfway between the curtain side fold and the first line of stitching.

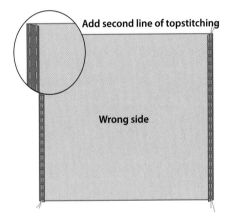

Add second line of topstitching

Wrong side

3 Form the casing.
- Clean finish the top edge of the curtain by zigzagging or serging.
- Turn under 2" along the top edge and press.

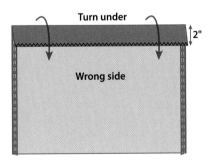

Turn under

2"

Wrong side

• Stitch 1⅝" from the folded edge using Jeans Stitch Thread.

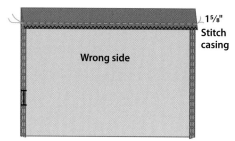

1⅝"
Stitch casing

4 Hem the curtain.
 • Turn under ½" along the bottom edge and press.
 • Turn under another ½" and press.
 • Stitch close to the inside folded edge.

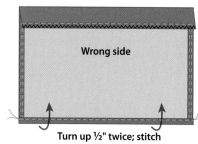

Turn up ½" twice; stitch

• Add another line of topstitching halfway between the curtain bottom and the first line of stitching.

Wrong side

Add second line of topstitching

5 Add the pockets.
 • Position the pockets on the right side of the curtain. You can follow the layout pictured or change it to suit your needs. For example, you might want to use only two pockets, or even just one.
 • Topstitch each pocket in place with two lines of stitching, following the pocket's original stitching lines.

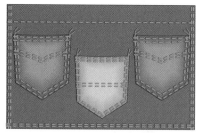

Stitch pockets to right side

6 Add the belt loops.
 • Check to ensure that the ends of each belt loop are turned under approximately ½". If not, turn under the ends ½" and press.

Make sure ends are turned under

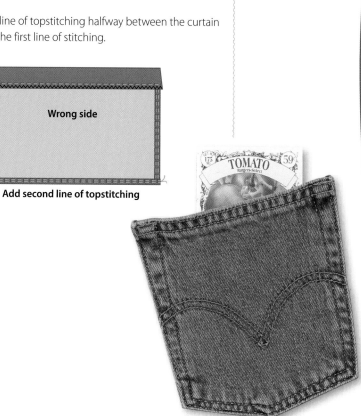

• Position the belt loops on the curtain, spacing them evenly apart.

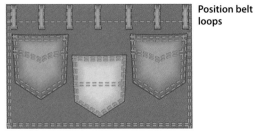

Position belt loops

• Bartack the ends of each belt loop to secure the loops in place.

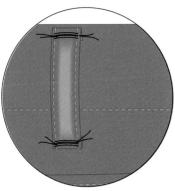

Bartack belt loops in place

Motivating Memo The number of belt loops you need depends on how far apart you space them. For the pictured curtain, we used nine belt loops and spaced them approximately 2" apart.

❼ To hang the curtain, use either the casing formed by the belt loops or the casing sewn into the fabric.

Nugget of Inspiration

This curtain is bursting with creative potential! For example, hang it from the sewn casing with a curtain rod and thread a handkerchief "belt" through the belt loops. Or make a custom curtain rod by gluing a leather belt to a curtain rod and use the belt loops to hang the curtain. As you can see, there are lots of ways to play up this curtain. You can also use the pockets for storing items such as pens, hair accessories, or small toys.

Throw Pillows

Another staple of home decorating, pillows are versatile and surprisingly easy to make. Stitch up a couple of pillows to accent a couch or throw several pillows on your bed to add a quick splash of color or personality. Use decorator fabrics or experiment with more unconventional fabrics such as animal skins, sequins, and fake fur to create pillows that reflect your true spirit, whether you're mild or wild!

Basic Pillow

Basic Pillow Instructions

1 Cut the fabric.
- To determine the fabric dimensions, start with the size of your pillow form. Pillow forms are available in many sizes. We'll give details for 14", 16", 18", and 20" sizes.
- To determine the fabric width, add 1" to the pillow size. For example:
  - 14" pillow form = 15" fabric width
  - 16" pillow form = 17" fabric width
  - 18" pillow form = 19" fabric width
  - 20" pillow form = 21" fabric width
- To determine fabric length, double the pillow size and add 10". For example:
  - 14" pillow form, 14" + 14" + 10" = 38"
  - 16" pillow form, 16" + 16" + 10" = 42"
  - 18" pillow form, 18" + 18" + 10" = 46"
  - 20" pillow form, 20" + 20" + 10" = 50"
- For example, for a 14" pillow form, cut a 15" x 38" rectangle of fabric.

2 Clean finish all four edges of the rectangle by zigzagging or serging.

3 Place the fabric wrong side up on the work surface.

4 Turn under 4" on each short edge; pin.

5 Fold the fabric in half with right sides together, overlapping the folded edges 2"; pin.

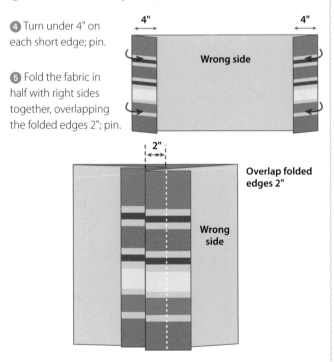

Overlap folded edges 2"

Motivating Memo You can position the stacked facings in the center of the pillow or off to one side.

6 Position the pillow facings in the desired location and pin. Stitch the top and bottom edges of the pillow using ½" seams.

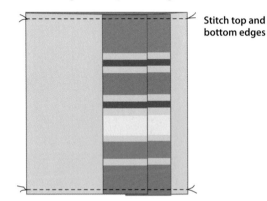

Stitch top and bottom edges

7 Turn the pillow right side out. Insert the pillow form.

8 *Optional:* Attach clasps to the pillow facings.
- Place the eye sections of the clasps on the overlap, positioning each section so the eye extends slightly past the fabric edge. Space the sections apart as desired.
- Stitch each eye section in place, stitching at the top and bottom.
- Position the hook sections on the pillow, aligning each with its corresponding eye section. Stitch in place.

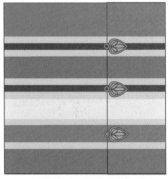

Position eye sections

Position and stitch hook sections

Variation 1: Reverse Pillow with Buttons

Note: This pillow is called "reverse" because the wrong side of the fabric shows on the facings. When choosing fabrics, keep in mind that both the right and wrong sides of the fabric will show on the pillow. Use either side as the right side.

1 Determine the yardage and cut fabric as detailed in Step 1 for the Basic Pillow.

2 Clean finish all four edges of the rectangle by zigzagging or serging.

3 Place the fabric right side up on the work surface.

4 Turn under 2" on each short edge and press. Fold under another 2" on each short edge and press.

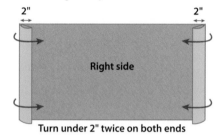

Turn under 2" twice on both ends

⑤ Edgestitch along both short edges to create the pillow facing.

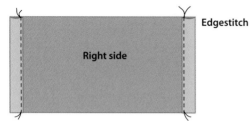

Edgestitch

Right side

⑥ Sew buttonholes and buttons on the facing.
 • Mark a line on one of the facings, approximately 1" from the folded edge.

▼ **Mark 1" from folded edge**

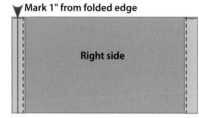

Right side

 • Determine the number of buttonholes, spacing them approximately 3" apart.
 • Stitch the buttonholes along the marked center line.

Stitch buttonholes

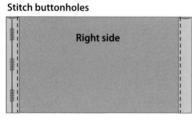

Right side

 • Open the buttonholes.
 • Fold the fabric in half with wrong sides together, overlapping the facings 2". Pin.

2"

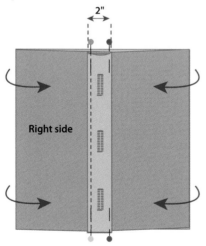

Right side

Overlap facings; pin

 • Mark the button positions on the second facing directly under each buttonhole. Unpin the facings.
 • Stitch the buttons in place.

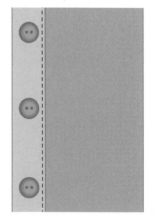

 • Button the top and bottom buttons. Turn the pillow wrong side out.

⑦ Complete the pillow.
 • Pin the stacked pillow facings in place.
 • Position the stacked facings in the center of the pillow or off to one side.
 • Stitch the top and bottom edges of the pillow.
 • Unbutton the top and bottom buttons. Press the seams open.
 • Turn the pillow right side out and insert the pillow form.

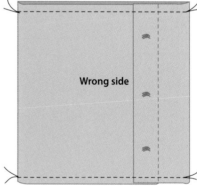

Wrong side

Stitch top and bottom edges

Variation 2: Reverse Pillow with Knot Buttons

1️⃣ Follow Steps 1 through 4 as detailed for the Reverse Pillow with Buttons.

2️⃣ Prepare the buttons and loops.

Cut one 2" x 45" strip for the loops and button knots.

• Fold the strip in half with right sides together, meeting the lengthwise edges.

Wrong side

Fold

• Stitch along the lengthwise edge, using a ½" seam.

• Turn the strip right side out using a Fasturn tool. This handy product will save you time and energy.

 - Select a Fasturn cylinder that slips easily inside the fabric tube. Insert the cylinder inside the stitched tube and press the seam open. Wrap and fold one end of the tube tightly over the end of the cylinder.

- Insert the wire into the cylinder from the handle end. Turn the hook clockwise so the hook goes through the fabric.

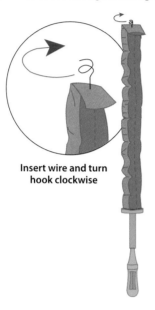

Insert wire and turn hook clockwise

- Gently pull the wire back through the cylinder, turning the tube right side out. Do not turn the hook, or it may release from the fabric.

- When the turned tube reaches the lower opening in the cylinder, release the hook by turning it counterclockwise. Complete turning by pulling the fabric.

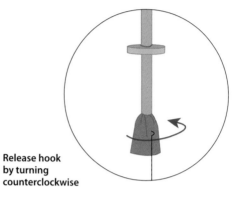

Release hook by turning counterclockwise

- Press the strip, placing the seam at one edge.
• Subcut the strip into three 7" long strips and three 8" long strips.

❸ Attach the knotted buttons.
• Tie a double knot at the center of each 8" strip.

• Position the raw edges of the knots under one folded edge, spacing them approximately 3" to 3½" apart. Baste the knots in place.

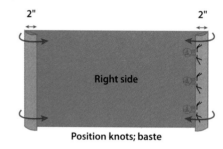

2"   2"

Right side

Position knots; baste

Motivating Memo The distance between the knots will depend on the size of the pillow form you're using. We used a 16" pillow form. If your pillow form is bigger or smaller, adjust the distance between the knots accordingly.

- Edgestitch along the fold to create a pillow facing and secure the knots.

Stitch along fold

❹ Attach the button loops.
- Fold each 7" long strip in half, meeting the short ends to form loops.

Fold in half

- Position the loops on the pillow, aligning them with the knotted buttons.
  - Fold the fabric with wrong sides together, overlapping the facings. Mark the loop positions directly opposite the knotted buttons.

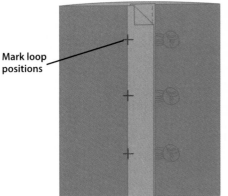

Mark loop positions

- Place the raw edges of the loops under the fold of the pillow facing. Baste the raw edges in place. Fold the loop over the facing and pin.

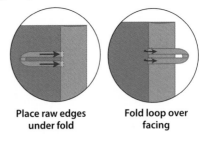

Place raw edges under fold   **Fold loop over facing**

  - Repeat, positioning and pinning the remaining two loops.
- Edgestitch along the folded edge of the facing and the button loops.

Stitch facing and loops in place

- Button the top and bottom buttons. Turn the pillow wrong side out.

❺ Complete the pillow as detailed in Step 7 for the Reverse Pillow with Buttons.

Pajama Pants and Tote

Walk through any clothing store, especially around the holidays, and you're sure to see sets of pajama pants packaged inside matching totes. Well, you now have the skills to make these sets yourself! Start by purchasing a pajama pants pattern. Practically every pattern company has one. Then follow these simple instructions to whip them up faster than you can say "Sweet Dreams."

Pajama Instructions

Note: *All seams are ⅝" unless otherwise stated.*

1 Cut out the pattern following the layout on the guide sheet. Remember to use the correct layout for the width of your fabric, and the nap layout if you're using a napped fabric or fabric with a one-way design.

Motivating Memo If your fabric looks similar on both the right and wrong sides, mark the right side of each fabric piece with a safety pin or piece of Sewer's Fix-it Tape or masking tape.

2 Before stitching any of the seams, press under the casing width (generally 1¼") using the Ezy-Hem Gauge. This establishes the position for the casing and sets the memory for turning under the casing.

Press casing

DRITZ EZY-HEM

3 Prepare each pant leg.
- Unfold the pressed casing.
- Meet the front and back pant legs with right sides together.
- Stitch the side seam and inseam on one pant leg.

Wrong side

Stitch side seam and inseam

- Press the seams flat, then open.
- Finish each seam edge by zigzagging or serging.
- Stitch the inseam on the second pant leg.
- Stitch the side seam on the second pant leg, beginning at the lower edge. Stop and backstitch at the pressed casing line, then advance the thread and stitch the final ¼" of the seam. This leaves an opening for inserting the elastic or for replacing the elastic in the future.

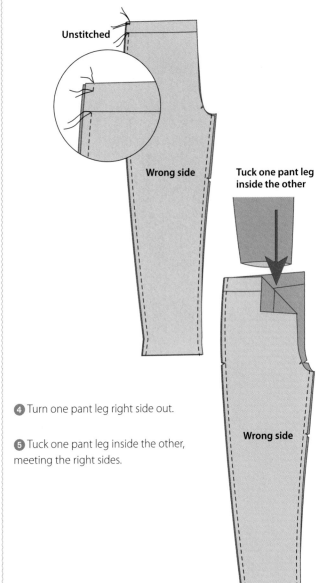

Unstitched

Wrong side

Tuck one pant leg inside the other

Wrong side

4 Turn one pant leg right side out.

5 Tuck one pant leg inside the other, meeting the right sides.

6 Stitch the front and back crotch seams in one operation. For reinforcement, restitch the seam close to the original stitching.

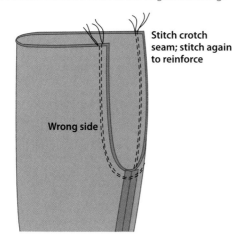

Stitch crotch seam; stitch again to reinforce

Wrong side

7 Construct the casing.
- Machine baste the seam allowances to the pants in the casing area for about 3" from the upper edge for easier insertion of elastic.

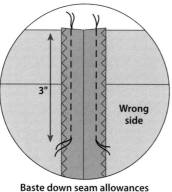

3"

Wrong side

Baste down seam allowances

- Clean finish the top edge of the pants by zigzagging, serging, or turning under the raw edge ¼".
- Fold the casing to the wrong side along the fold line. Stitch close to the folded edge. This row of stitching helps prevent the elastic from twisting and turning in the casing.

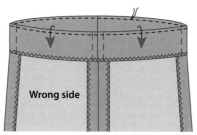

Wrong side

Fold casing down; stitch close to folded edge

- Add a second row of stitching near the cut edge of the casing.

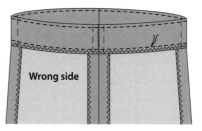

Wrong side

8 Insert the elastic in the casing.
- Cut a length of elastic approximately 2" smaller than the waistline measurement. Place the elastic around your waistline before inserting it in the garment to ensure it's comfortable. Adjust as needed.
- Zigzag one end of the elastic to a sturdy woven fabric scrap (for example, denim) that is wider than the elastic. This helps prevent the elastic from being drawn into the casing.

Zigzag elastic to fabric scrap

- Attach an E/Z Feeder Guide or safety pin to the unstitched end of the elastic. Thread the elastic through the opening, being careful not to twist or turn the elastic.

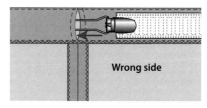

Wrong side

Insert elastic

- Join the ends of the elastic.
  - After the elastic is threaded through the casing, butt the unstitched end against the first end of the elastic. Zigzag through the elastic and fabric several times.

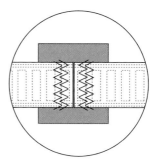

- Trim away the extra woven fabric. This eliminates the bulk of the elastic joining.

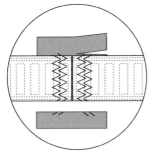

• Evenly distribute the fullness. (The elastic will slip through the opening in the seam.) Stitch in the ditch, sewing in the well of the seam at each side seam to keep the elastic evenly distributed.

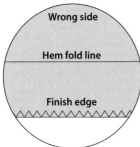

Stitch in the ditch at seamlines

Right side

• Remove the basting stitches.

⑨ Hem the pants.
  • Turn up the hem (usually 1¼") on the lower edge. Press.
  • Unfold the hem and zigzag, serge, or turn under the raw edges ¼".

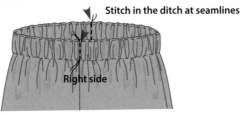

Wrong side

Hem fold line

Finish edge

• Refold the hem and topstitch 1" from the fold. Press.

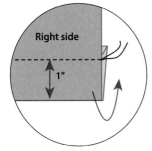

Right side

1"

Fold up hem and topstitch

Pajama Tote Instructions

Whip up a quick tote to match your pajama pants. Use the same fabric you used for the pants or choose a coordinating fabric. Construction is simple, and the tote makes a perfect carrying case/gift bag for the pants.

Finished size: approximately 11" x 11"

Note: *All seams are ½" unless otherwise stated.*

❶ Cut the fabric (you'll need approximately ½ yard).
  • Tote body, 12" x 24" rectangle
  • Tie, 2" x 30" strip

❷ Construct the tote body.
  • Clean finish each edge of the 12" x 24" rectangle by zigzagging or serging.
  • Fold the rectangle in half, meeting the 12" edges. Stitch one side seam, starting from the top and stitching toward the fold.

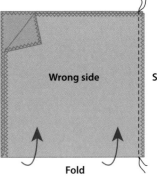

Wrong side

Stitch side seam

Fold

• Press the seam flat, then open.
• Press the top edges down 1¼" to form the casing.

Fold down casing

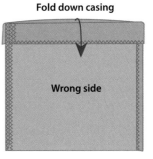

Wrong side

• Unfold the casing. Pin the remaining unstitched side seam.

- Stitch the side seam, starting at the top and stitching toward the fold. Stitch 1¼", then backstitch. Stitch the rest of the seam, beginning ¾" below the fold.

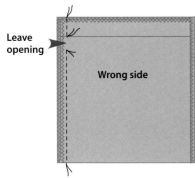

Leave opening

Wrong side

- Press the seam flat, then open.
- Edgestitch around the casing opening.

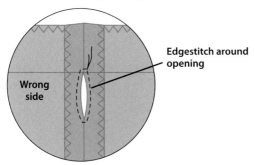

Wrong side

Edgestitch around opening

- Refold and pin the casing. Stitch 1" from the fold.

1"

Wrong side

- Form a gusset at the lower edge.
  - At each corner, fold the fabric so the side seam stacks on top of the lower edge fold, forming a triangle.
  - Measure and mark a line 1½" from the corner.
  - Stitch along the line. Repeat on the opposite corner.

1½"

3 Create the tie.
  - Clean finish 2" edges of the 2" x 30" strip by zigzagging or serging.
  - Fold the strip in half with right sides together, meeting the lengthwise edges.

Fold

- Stitch along the lengthwise edge.

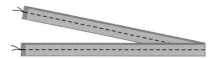

  - Turn the tie right side out using a Fasturn as detailed in Step 2 for the Reverse Pillow with Knot Buttons, pages 124-125.
  - *Optional:* Edgestitch along each edge of the tie, stitching one continuous seam and pivoting at the corners.

Edgestitch

  - Insert the tie into the casing.
  - Attach an E/Z Feeder Guide or safety pin to the tie.
  - Thread the tie through the opening, being careful not to twist or turn the tie.

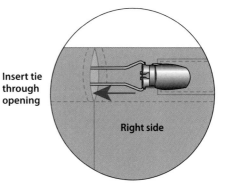

Insert tie through opening

Right side

- Knot the two ends of the tie together.

Gift Bags

Share your creativity with your friends and family by creating unique fabric gift bags. Whether you're giving a bottle of wine, a bottle of gourmet vinegar or olives, a small book or toy, or a CD, wrap the item in a fabric bag for an impressive gift. The lucky recipient is sure to discover many uses for the bag.

Basic Gift Bag/ Wine Tote

Basic Gift Bag/Wine Tote Instructions

Finished size: approximately 7" x 15¾"

1 Cut one 8" x 42" rectangle of fabric. Clean finish all the edges by zigzagging or serging.

2 Construct the bag.
- Fold the fabric in half with right sides together, meeting the 8" edges. Stitch both side seams, using ½" seams.

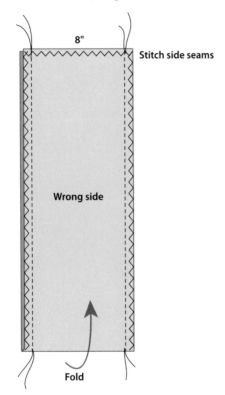

8"

Stitch side seams

Wrong side

Fold

- Press the seams flat.
- Form a gusset at the lower edge.

- Fold up the bottom edge approximately 2¼".
- Stitch the gusset in place, following the side seam stitching lines.

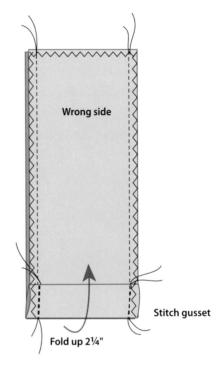

Wrong side

Stitch gusset

Fold up 2¼"

3 Complete the bag.
- Turn under and press 3" at the top edge, forming the hem. Stitch close to the cut edge.

Stitch casing

Wrong side

- Turn the bag right side out.
- Insert a bottle of wine and tie a cord with a tassel around the bag.

Variation 1: Gift Bag with Draw Cord

Variation 1: Gift Bag with Draw Cord Instructions

Finished size: approximately 7" x 10"

1 Cut a rectangle of fabric 8" x 22". Clean finish all the edges by zigzagging or serging.

2 Construct the bag.
- Fold the fabric in half with right sides together, meeting the 8" edges.
- Stitch one side seam, using a ½" seam. Press the seam flat, then open.

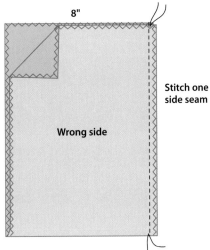

8"

Stitch one side seam

Wrong side

3 Form the casing.
- On the remaining side edge, stitch 1" down from the top raw edges; backstitch. Stitch the rest of the seam, beginning ¾" below the backstitching. Press the seam open.

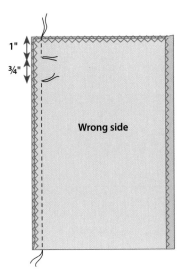

1"

¾"

Wrong side

- Edgestitch around the casing opening.

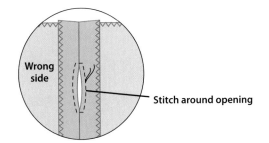

Wrong side

Stitch around opening

- Turn under and press 1" along the top edge, forming the casing.

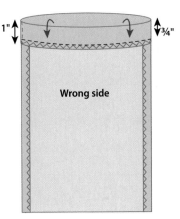

1"

¾"

Wrong side

- Stitch approximately ¾" from the folded edge.
- Insert a draw cord through the casing. Attach a cord lock at the ends. Knot both ends of the cord.

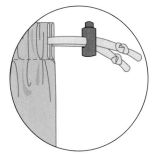

Variation 2: CD Envelope with Flap

Variation 2: CD Envelope with Flap Instructions

Finished size: approximately 6½" x 7"

1 Cut a rectangle of fabric 7" x 34". Clean finish all the edges by zigzagging or serging.

2 Construct the envelope.
- Fold the fabric in half with right sides together, meeting the 7" edges.
- Mark the center of the top edge with a ¼" line.

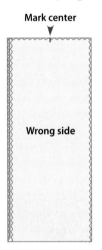

Mark center

Wrong side

- Measure and mark 3" down from the top edge on both sides. Draw ¼" lines at each mark.

3"   3"

Wrong side

- Draw lines connecting the center top mark to the inner edge of each ¼" side mark.
  - Straight stitch along the lines.

Connect marks

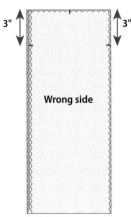

Wrong side

- Trim the seam allowances to ¼". Clip to each corner. Press the seams flat.

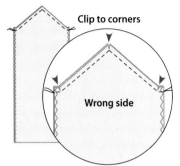

Clip to corners

Wrong side

- Turn the envelope right side out and press.
- Bring the bottom fold to meet the base of the flap, aligning the fold with the ¼" extensions.
- Stitch both side edges, using ¼" seams. Press.

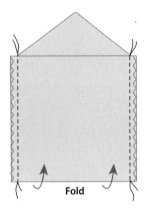

Fold

- Turn the envelope right side out.
- Use a decorative pin as a closure.

Nugget of Inspiration

Just for fun, walk around your favorite clothing store and notice how many of the garments you are now able to sew. Pajama pants? Simple skirts with elastic waistbands? You can totally do that. And you'll do it in the colors and fabrics of your choice. Your wardrobe will soon be full of designer originals! After the clothing, take a stroll through your favorite home décor store. Look at all the things that you are now able to sew. Throw pillows and curtains? You can make those. And you'll have the fun of picking exactly the fabrics you want.

Refresh Your Memory

- **6" hem gauge**. Sewing gauge with a double-pointed slide to guide in marking hems, pleats, buttons, and buttonhole placements. The sliding pointer makes it easy to get even measurements.

- **Backstitch**. To secure stitches at the beginning and end of each seam, which prevents them from coming out. Sew two or three stitches, adjust the machine to stitch in reverse, sew two or three stitches, and then proceed with the seam.

- **Bamboo pointer and creaser**. Use the pointed end of this tool to get sharp, crisp corners when turning collars, cuffs, lapels, and appliqués. Use the curved beveled end to temporarily press open seams or to shape curved edges (for example, on a round pillow).

- **Bartack**. To stitch in place to secure facings or sew-on buttons.

- **Basting**. Long running stitches used to hold two or more layers of fabric in position. The temporary stitches are often removed after the final stitching is done.

- **Bias**. Diagonal line between the lengthwise and crosswise threads on a fabric. A true bias lies at a 45° angle to the selvage and has more stretch than lengthwise or crosswise grains.

- **Blades**. Parts of a serger that cut the fabric as it is stitched. One blade remains stationary while a second blade moves up and down in synchronization with the needle(s).

- **Blind hem stitch**. Machine stitch formed using a special blind hem foot and stitch setting. The machine makes several straight stitches followed by one zigzag stitch, repeated along the entire hem.

- **Bobbin**. Case that holds the lower thread in a conventional sewing machine.

- **Bodkin**. Tool used to insert ribbon, lace, or elastic into a garment casing.

- **Braided elastic**. The most economical of elastics. Because it narrows when stretched, it should only be used in casings.

- **Buttonhole cutter and block**. Set of tools used to open buttonholes for a neat, professional look. The cutter has a hardwood handle with a hardened steel blade; the wooden block comes in various shapes.

- **Casing**. Channel formed by two layers of fabric connected by two or more rows of stitching, in which elastic, a drawstring, or a curtain rod is inserted.

- **Chalk or chalk wheel**. Tool used for marking darts, pleats, and button or buttonhole placement on fabric.

- **Clean finish**. To finish the cut edges of a seam by zigzagging, serging, or turning under and stitching a narrow hem.

- **Clips**. Short cuts made perpendicular to the seamline after joining two garment pieces. Clips are used to help curved pieces lie flat after being turned.

- **Cone serger thread**. Two-ply thread used primarily in sergers. Because this thread is lighter weight than all-purpose thread, it reduces bulk at the seamline.

- **Crosswise grain**. Yarns that run across the fabric from one selvage to the other. Crosswise yarns stretch more than lengthwise yarns. Most projects are cut with the crosswise yarns going around.

- **Dart**. Triangular fold of fabric with wide ends tapering to a point. Darts help shape a garment so it fits around curves such as body contours.

- **Double needles**. Used only on zigzag machines. Two needles joined together at one shank; used for decorative stitching. The needle threads stitch two parallel lines, while the bobbin thread zigzags between the two needle threads. Double needles are also known as twin needles.

• **Easing**. The process of gathering extra fullness in one piece of fabric to make it fit with another piece. This technique is used often when setting in cap sleeves.

• **Edgestitch**. Straight stitching close to an edge.

• **Ezy-Hem Gauge**. Lightweight metal gauge used to mold straight or curved hems while measuring accurately, in one easy step. The gauge also prevents pressing over the cut edge of the hem, which could leave an imprint on the right side of the fabric.

• **Facing**. Garment piece that covers and encloses a raw edge.

• **Feed dogs**. Teeth-like grippers nestled in the throat plate of a sewing machine or serger. The feed dogs move back and forth to feed the fabric through the machine as stitches are formed.

• **Finger press**. To apply pressure to an area by compressing the fabric layers with your fingers.

• **Full fuse**. Interfacing the entire fabric piece. Cut interfacing to the pattern size instead of trimming away the seam allowances.

• **Fusible interfacings**. Interfacings treated with a special heat-activated resin. When pressed with an iron, a fusible interfacing is bonded permanently to the wrong side of the fashion fabric.

• **Gathering**. Used to pull fabric into soft folds when joining a larger section of fabric to a smaller one. Accomplished by stitching a wide zigzag over heavier cord or thread, or stitching several rows of basting stitches, then pulling up the cord or bobbin threads to finished size.

• **Grading**. Cutting each enclosed seam allowance a different width to reduce bulk. Facing seams are generally trimmed to ¼" and garment seams to ⅜".

• **Grain**. Lengthwise and crosswise threads of a woven fabric. The lengthwise grain is parallel to the selvage and has the least amount of stretch. The crosswise grain is perpendicular to the selvage and has a little more give.

• **Grainline**. Indicated on a pattern by an arrow that aligns with the lengthwise or crosswise grain of the fabric.

• **Gridded cutting mat**. Mat made of a special "self-healing" material that is not damaged by the blade of a rotary cutter; often marked with horizontal and vertical lines for ease in measuring. The cutting mat protects the work surface and is a must when using a rotary cutter.

• **Gridded ruler**. Heavyweight transparent plastic ruler marked with horizontal and vertical lines for ease in measuring. The gridded ruler is used with a rotary cutter and cutting mat.

• **Hem**. Technique for finishing a piece of fabric by turning under a cut edge and stitching (or fusing) in place.

• **Interfacing**. Second layer of lightweight fabric added to the inside of a garment to add shape and body.

• **Knit fabric**. Fabric created by interlocking loops of yarn – one loop of yarn pulled through another loop. Most knits stretch. Examples of knit fabrics include interlock, sweatshirt fleece, and sweater knits.

• **Lengthwise grain**. Yarns that run the same direction as the selvages. Lengthwise yarns are usually stronger and heavier than crosswise yarns. Most projects are cut with the lengthwise yarns going up and down.

• **Lock stitch**. Two or three stitches sewn in one place to secure threads.

• **Loopers**. Devices found on sergers that handle the lower threads. Sergers have upper and lower loopers. Loopers do not go through the fabric. Instead, they interlock the threads in a knit-like fashion.

• **Lower looper thread**. Serger thread on the right on most sergers. This thread does not pass through the fabric. It passes underneath the fabric, catching the needle thread on the left and the upper looper thread on the right.

• **Multi-sized pattern**. Pattern with several different sizes in one pattern, for example, sizes ranging from 8 to 12. Each pattern piece has cutting lines for all the sizes included in the pattern.

• **Multi-zigzag**. Variation of a machine zigzag stitch formed by sewing three stitches in each direction. It is often used when a stretch stitch or understitching is recommended.

• **Nap**. The pile and hair on fabrics that have a definite "up" and "down." Napped fabrics include camel's hair, mohair, brushed denim, corduroy, velvet, and sweatshirt fleece.

• **Nip**. ¼" clip cut into a seam allowance prior to sewing. A nip marks a notch, dart, tuck, fold line, or other important point on the fabric.

• **Nonroll elastic**. Type of knitted elastic that retains its shape and stays flat when stretched.

• **Nonwoven fabric**. Fabric formed from fibers forced together with heat, moisture, and pressure. Examples of nonwoven fabrics include synthetic suede, felt, and many interfacings.

• **Notch**. Single-, double-, or triple-diamond markings found on sewing patterns that are used to match garment pieces accurately.

• **Notions**. Items you need to complete a sewing project, such as zippers, buttons, hooks and eyes, and thread.

• **One-way design**. Fabric design that has a definite top and bottom.

- **One-way layout**. Method of placing all pattern pieces for a project with their tops facing in a single direction to avoid directional shading. One-way layouts are important when cutting napped fabrics (such as velvet and corduroy) and many knits, as well as fabrics with one-way designs; also referred to as "with nap" layout.

- **Overlock seam**. The most common stitch produced by a serger, also often used to finish seams stitched on a conventional sewing machine.

- **Paper-backed fusible web**. Fusible web with removable paper backing. Used for fusing hems and appliqués; you can trace on the paper backing.

- **Pinking shears**. Shears with special serrated blades that cut a decorative zigzag edge.

- **Pins**. Necessary for any sewing project, pins temporarily hold layers of fabric together.

- **Pleat**. Fold of fabric similar to a dart, but with no point at the end.

- **Press cloth**. Piece of lightweight fabric placed between the iron and fabric when pressing. It protects the fabric surface from damage and keeps the bottom of your iron clean when fusing interfacing.

- **Presser foot**. Part of the sewing machine or serger that holds that fabric against the feed dogs as the stitches are formed.

- **Pressing ham**. Pressing tool with a large curved surface. Use a ham to press curved areas such as darts or curved seams so they keep their shapes.

- **Pressing seams flat**. First step of the two-step procedure for pressing all seams. Press the seam flat, then press it open or to one side.

- **Prewashing**. Process of washing and drying washable fabric prior to cutting and sewing. Prewashing reduces shrinkage in the final project, removes resins from the fabric, and helps to prevent skipped stitches during sewing.

- **Pucker**. Undesirable bunching of fabric that usually occurs where two seams of different lengths are joined, such as the seam that joins the sleeve cap and the armhole.

- **Quarter marks**. Points indicated with pins or a washable marker to divide fabric into four equal parts. Quarter marks are used to position and distribute fabric evenly when sewing ribbing or elastic, for example, to the waist, neckline, or the sleeves of a garment.

- **Ribbing**. Knit fabric used to finish the neckline, waist, and wrists of garments.

- **Right side**. Side of fabric that shows on the outside. With printed fabrics, the design is printed on the right side. With napped fabrics, the nap is pronounced on the right side.

- **Rotary cutter**. Special fabric cutting tool that looks and works like a pizza cutter. Used in combination with a special cutting mat and gridded ruler, it is used to cut one or more layers of fabric accurately.

- **Scallop shears**. Shears with special blades that cut a rounded scalloped edge on fabric.

- **Scissors**. Cutting tools with blades less than 6" long and have identical handle bows for the finger and thumb. Scissors are perfect for trimming, clipping, and crafts.

- **Seam allowance**. Distance between the cutting line and seamline; usually $5/8$".

- **Seam ripper**. Used for removing stitching mistakes. A seam ripper has a special sharp point that slides under and cuts the thread.

- **Seam roll**. Pressing tool used to press open seams. The rounded surface of a seam roll prevents the imprint of the seam edges from showing on the right side of the fabric. You can make a seam roll by tightly rolling and taping a magazine and covering it with fabric or a terry towel.

- **Seamline**. Stitching line followed when sewing a seam. On pattern pieces, it usually appears as a broken line inside the solid cutting line.

- **Selvage**. Tightly woven finished edges of fabric. Selvages do not ravel.

- **Serged seams**. Seams stitched on a serger with a 3 thread or 3/4-thread overlock stitch.

- **Serger**. Special sewing machine that uses three, four, or more threads instead of the two threads used on a conventional sewing machine. It stitches a seam, finishes the raw edges, and cuts off excess fabric all at the same time.

- **Sewer's Fix-it Tape**. This easy to remove tape is an essential and versatile sewing tool. Use it to tape patterns; you can write on it and iron over it, and the pattern remains tissue soft. It also works as a ½" stitching guide when inserting zippers.

- **Shank**. Wrapped thread that connects a button to a project. Button shanks make it possible for the buttonhole placket to fit under buttons without puckering.

- **Sharpening stone**. Tool used to sharpen shears and scissors periodically to ensure clean-cut edges.

- **Shears**. Cutting tools with blades longer than 6" and different-sized handle bows or loops (a small loop for the thumb and a larger loop for two or more fingers). Shears are perfect for cutting out fabric.

- **Sleeve board**. Pressing tool with a free arm for pressing small openings and hard to reach areas such as sleeves and pant legs.

- **Stitch in the ditch**. Stitching in the well or groove of a seam on the right side of the project, through all thicknesses to secure sections and keep them in place.

- **Tape measure**. Tape used for larger measurements such as measuring fabric grainline and determining pattern size. Choose a 60" long tape made of durable, nonstretching material with metal or plastic on the ends to prevent fraying. Some tape measures have markings on both sides in metric and American measurements.

- **Test swatch**. Small square of fusible interfacing and fabric used to determine the suitability and fusing time required for your selected fabric and interfacing.

- **Thread**. All-purpose thread made of cotton covered polyester or 100% polyester is the type most often used for machine sewing. Available in a wide variety of colors, this thread works with all types of fabrics for all-purpose sewing.

- **Topstitch**. Decorative straight stitch a uniform distance from an edge on the right side of fabric.

- **Tracing wheel and paper**. Tools used to transfer pattern marks to fabric. Tracing wheels may have pointed (serrated) or smooth edges. Serrated edges make a dotted line, but may leave holes in the pattern. Smooth edges make a solid line, which puts more marks on the fabric. Tracing paper is specially designed for use with tracing wheels on fabric.

- **Trimming**. Reducing the width of a stitched seam to eliminate bulk.

- **Unbacked fusible web**. Fusible web with no backing. Often used for fusing hems and appliqués.

- **Understitch**. Pressing seam allowances toward a facing or under collar, then stitching close to the seam on the facing to prevent the facing from rolling to the right side.

- **Universal point needles**. All-purpose sewing machine needles used for general sewing on knit and woven fabrics.

- **Upper looper thread**. Second or third thread from the right on a serger. This thread does not pass through the fabric. Instead, it passes over the surface of the fabric, catching the needle thread on the left and the lower looper thread on the right.

- **Water- or air-soluble marking pens**. Marking tools used to transfer pattern markings to fabric. The marks from water-soluble pens will disappear after being washed; the marks from air-soluble pens will disappear within 12 to 48 hours, depending upon the humidity in the air.

- **Woven fabric**. Fabric made by interlacing threads over and under one another. Examples of woven fabrics include denim, corduroy, muslin, and broadcloth.

- **Wrapped corner**. Sewing technique used to eliminate bulk in corners.

- **Wrong side**. Side of fabric that doesn't show; it faces the inside. On printed fabrics, the unprinted side is the wrong side. On napped fabrics, the nap is less pronounced on the wrong side.

- **Yardage**. Amount of fabric needed to complete a project. Fabric is measured in yards or meters.

Charts

Yardage Conversion

If the width of fabric you want to buy differs from the fabric width on the pattern envelope, use the conversion chart below to determine how much you should buy. Remember to buy extra fabric if you're enlarging the pattern or buying fabric with a large-scale or a one-way design.

Fabric Width		**Yardage**										
32"	1⅞	2¼	2½	2¾	3⅛	3⅜	3¾	4	4⅜	4⅝	5	5¼
35"-36"	1¾	2	2¼	2½	2⅞	3⅛	3⅜	3¾	4¼	4½	4¾	5
44"-45"	1⅜	1⅝	1¾	2⅛	2¼	2½	2¾	2⅞	3⅛	3⅜	3⅝	3⅞
52"-54"	1⅛	1⅜	1½	1¾	1⅞	2	2¼	2⅜	2⅝	2¾	2⅞	3⅛
58"-60"	1	1¼	1⅜	1⅝	1¾	1⅞	2	2¼	2⅜	2⅝	2¾	2⅞

Metric Conversion – Yards to Meters

Yards	Meters	Yards	Meters	Yards	Meters	Yards	Meters	Yards	Meters
⅛	0.15	2⅛	1.95	4⅛	3.80	6⅛	5.60	8⅛	7.45
¼	0.25	2¼	2.10	4¼	3.90	6¼	5.75	8¼	7.55
⅜	0.35	2⅜	2.20	4⅜	4.00	6⅜	5.85	8⅜	7.70
½	0.50	2½	2.30	4½	4.15	6½	5.95	8½	7.80
⅝	0.60	2⅝	2.40	4⅝	4.25	6⅝	6.10	8⅝	7.90
¾	0.70	2¾	2.55	4¾	4.35	6¾	6.20	8¾	8.00
⅞	0.80	2⅞	2.65	4⅞	4.50	6⅞	6.30	8⅞	8.15
1	0.95	3	2.75	5	4.60	7	6.40	9	8.25
1⅛	1.05	3⅛	2.90	5⅛	4.70	7⅛	6.55	9⅛	8.35
1¼	1.15	3¼	3.00	5¼	4.80	7¼	6.65	9¼	8.50
1⅜	1.30	3⅜	3.10	5⅜	4.95	7⅜	6.75	9⅜	8.60
1½	1.40	3½	3.20	5½	5.05	7½	6.90	9½	8.70
1⅝	1.50	3⅝	3.35	5⅝	5.15	7⅝	7.00	9⅝	8.80
1¾	1.60	3¾	3.45	5¾	5.30	7¾	7.10	9¾	8.95
1⅞	1.75	3⅞	3.55	5⅞	5.40	7⅞	7.20	9/8	9.05
2	1.85	4	3.70	6	5.50	8	7.35	10	9.15

Metric Conversion – Inches to Centimeters

Inches	Centimeters	Inches	Centimeters	Inches	Centimeters	Inches	Centimeters	Inches	Centimeters
⅛	.3	3	7.5	13	33	26	66	39	99
¼	.6	3½	9	14	35.5	27	68.5	40	102
⅜	1	4	10	15	38	28	71	41	104
½	1.3	4½	11.5	16	40.5	29	73.5	42	107
⅝	1.5	5	12.5	17	43	30	76	43	109
¾	2	5½	14	18	46	31	78.5	44	112
⅞	2.2	6	15	19	48.5	32	81.5	45	115
1	2.5	7	18	20	51	33	84	46	117
1¼	3.2	8	20.5	21	53.5	34	86.5	47	120
1½	3.8	9	23	22	56	35	89	48	122
1¾	4.5	10	25.5	23	58.5	36	91.5	49	125
2	5	11	28	24	61	37	94	50	127
2½	6.3	12	30.5	25	63.5	38	96.5		

Index

EXPERT ADVICE *from* Nancy Zieman

Sewing With Nancy's Favorite Hints
20th Anniversary Edition
by Nancy Zieman

This necessity for every sewing room presents a collection of Nancy Zieman's favorite tips, hints, and techniques from the past two decades. You'll find tips for keeping your sewing room organized, Nancy's favorite notions, helpful sewing solutions, embroidery hints, quilting tips, and more! Relive the memories of the longest-running sewing program on public television with the nation's leading sewing authority!

Softcover • 8-1/4 x 10-7/8 • 144 pages
150 color photos
Item# NFTT • $19.95

Sewing With Nancy® 10-20-30 Minutes to Sew for Your Home
by Nancy Zieman

Offers more than 25 soft-furnishing projects for every room of the home that can be completed even by those who only have 10, 20, or 30 minutes to spare. You'll quickly learn to create a quilt for the bedroom, a table runner for the kitchen, a machine mat for the sewing room, crib sheets for baby's room, and much more! Nancy Zieman's step-by-step instructions will guide you through everything from choosing fabrics and supplies to a successful finished project.

Softcover • 8-1/4 x 10-7/8 • 96 pages
50 color photos, plus step-by-step instructions
Item# MNSYH • $16.95

Creative Kindness
People and Projects Making a Difference—and How You Can, Too
by Nancy Zieman with Gail Brown

Make a difference in the lives of those less fortunate. Meet real life volunteers and everyday heroes as they share their stories of generosity and caring support. Create twelve projects, including a care cloth, sleepers, a sleeping bag, and pillows suitable for crafters of all skill levels by following simple step-by-step instructions. Use your sewing, quilting, knitting, and crocheting skills to help others. Experience the contagious generosity of "from hands to hearts, with hope."

Softcover • 8-1/8 x 10-7/8 • 96 pages
color throughout
Item# CRKI • $12.99

Landscape Quilts for Kids
by Nancy Zieman and Natalie Sewell

Easily personalize a quilt for any child with the beauty of the outdoors-add names, favorite animals, and playful children to nature scenes. More than 10 quilting projects, perfect to give as gifts, are thoroughly explained with easy-to-follow instructions and full-color, step-by-step photos and illustrations-several pages of kids and animals of photo transfer quality are included! Plus, as a source of inspiration, large color photographs brilliantly display each finished project.

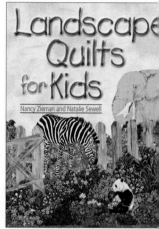

Softcover • 8-1/4 x 10-7/8 • 96 pages
100 color photos
Item# LQKI • $19.99

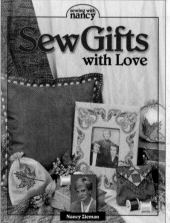

Sew Gifts With Love
by Nancy Zieman

Create gorgeous evening bags, picture frames, fleece throws, bathroom towels, jewelry baskets, and more. Give these wonderful creations away or keep them for yourself, either way, they will be treasured for years to come. Learn to incorporate unique designs, such as hearts, snowflakes, and pineapples, into everyday personal accessory and home décor items. Patterns, detailed illustrations, and step-by-step instructions ensure you complete projects successfully every time.

Softcover • 8-1/4 x 10-7/8 • 144 pages
100 color photos
Item# SGWL • $21.99